The Psychology of Lying and Detecting Lies

Bella DePaulo, Ph.D.

THE PSYCHOLOGY OF LYING AND DETECTING LIES
may be purchased for educational, business, or sales
promotional use. For information, contact the author.

DePaulo, Bella

    The psychology of lying and detecting lies

ISBN-13: **978-1986744423**

ISBN-10: **1986744426**

FIRST EDITION: March 2018

Printed in the United States of America

10 9 8 7 6 5 4 3 2 1

Also by BELLA DePAULO

- Singled Out: How Singles Are Stereotyped, Stigmatized, and Ignored, and Still Live Happily Ever After
- How We Live Now: Redesigning Home and Family in the 21st Century
- Alone: The Badass Psychology of People Who Like Being Alone
- The Best of Single Life
- Marriage vs. Single Life: How Science and the Media Got It So Wrong
- Singlism: What It Is, Why It Matters, and How to Stop It
- Single Parents and Their Children: The Good News No One Ever Tells You
- Single, No Children: Who Is Your Family?
- The Science of Marriage: What We Know That Just Isn't So
- Single with Attitude: Not Your Typical Take on Health and Happiness, Love and Money, Marriage and Friendship

- Behind the Door of Deceit: Understanding the Biggest Liars in Our Lives
- The Hows and Whys of Lies
- When the Truth Hurts: Lying to Be Kind
- The Lies We Tell and the Clues We Miss: Professional Papers
- Is Anyone Really Good at Detecting Lies? Professional Papers

- Friendsight: What Friends Know that Others Don't
- New Directions in Helping: Volumes 1, 2, and 3
- The Psychology of Dexter

CONTENTS IN BRIEF

CONTENTS

Preface

For the first two decades of my professional career, I studied the psychology of lying and detecting lies. I published more than 100 scholarly articles and chapters, including some of the best-known and most widely-cited papers in the field, before changing my focus to the study of people who are single. Still, I continue to write occasionally about liars and their lies.

At first, all my writings about deception appeared in scholarly journals or books, too often impenetrable to anyone not steeped in statistics and academic jargon. That's no longer true. I now write articles for publications such as the *Washington Post* and the *New York Times*, for blogs, and for books that can be read by curious people everywhere, regardless of their backgrounds.

THE PSYCHOLOGY OF LYING AND DETECTING LIES is a collection of 29 of my previously-published writings. Many of them appeared in the blogs I have been writing at Psychology Today (since 2008) and Psych Central (since 2011). It also includes a chapter on Dexter's lies that originally appeared in a book I edited, *The Psychology of Dexter*.

In the forty years I've been publishing, I don't think anything has been read by more people than an article I wrote for the *Washington Post* on December 8, 2017, "I study liars. I've never seen one like President Trump." This collection includes an overview of the main points of that article, along with some background about it that does not appear in the *Post*. I also included, for your amusement, a brief description of some of the incensed responses the article elicited.

THE PSYCHOLOGY OF LYING AND DETECTING LIES opens with some truths about lying that I have discovered over the many years I have spent studying the topic. I then profile ordinary liars, including their personalities and sex differences, before turning to the psychology of big-time liars.

The section on detecting deception, "Figuring Out When You Are Getting Duped," includes answers to some of the questions I have been asked most often. What are the cues to deception? Are we using the right cues when we try to figure out if someone is lying? How good are we at detecting other people's lies, when we have nothing to go by other than their words and their nonverbal cues? Is there such a thing as gut-level detection of deception? And, more philosophically, if you could know exactly what other people were thinking and feeling, would you want to?

The dynamics of lying and detecting lies in relationships gets a lot of attention in THE PSYCHOLOGY OF LYING AND DETECTING LIES. It has its own section. When I talk about relationships, I don't just mean romantic ones, so in that section you will learn about lying in all sorts of relationships, including our interactions with friends, family members, acquaintances, and even strangers. The findings are not always the ones you might intuit. For example, sometimes strangers know us better than our romantic partners do, at least when it comes to the detection of our lies.

When I published my first scholarly article about deception in 1979, "Telling lies," there was so little written on the topic in academic journals that the editor did something truly unusual: He asked me and my co-author, the esteemed Robert Rosenthal, to write a longer article than the one we submitted. He wanted us to set out a roadmap for future research on the psychology of lying and detecting lies.

Things have changed dramatically since then. Spurred on at least in part by 9/11 and the subsequent urgency of understanding when people might have something potentially catastrophic to hide, the field of deception is now a burgeoning one. Many books have been written, including some of my own. This collection is just a sampling of some of the shorter articles and chapters I have written over the years. I hope you enjoy it.

Bella DePaulo, Ph.D.
Summerland, CA
USA
BellaDePaulo.com

[Note to readers of the print version of this book: Words or phrases that are underlined will show up as links in the e-book version.]

I.

First, Some Truths about Lies

1.

6 Truths about Lies

Lying is easy; detecting lies is hard.

A recent story about human lie detectors boasted one of the rarest — and most accurate — subheading ever written on the topic: "The death of the dead give-away." So often, we hear instead about how this twitch or that manner or speaking or some other muscle movement is the new and shiny tell-tale clue to deceit. There are some clues to deception, but they are probabilistic cues, not dead give-aways.

In the spirit of truth-telling about lying, here are some everlasting truths about deception.

1. There is no perfect clue to deception. There is no behavior that always occurs when people are lying and never occurs any other time. The dead give-away is a ghost of a phenomenon that never did exist and never will. Pinocchio, your nose is toast!
2. There are no perfect human lie-detectors. There have been claims that some select people are "wizards" at detecting deception. Charlie Bond and I have cast some doubt on that claim. But there is one thing that even the believers in wizards will agree with me on: No one is right all the time about whether another person is lying.
3. Neuroscience will not provide the magic bullet of lie-detection. Brain scans, fMRI, neuroimaging and such are all the rage, but they will not offer perfect deception-detection capabilities either. Lies are too diverse for that. The emotions, cognitions, and self-presentational goals of different kinds of lies are just too different to support a single tell-tale brain

signature. Plus, it is not too practical to depend on this sort of expensive and unwieldy technology.

4. There will always be cultural hand-wringing about liars and their lies. Plagiarism, big-time lying, even scientific fraud all seems rampant these days. But check out the cultural critics of bye-gone times and I bet you will find some of the same laments about casual attitudes toward the truth.

5. People will never stop lying. Some people lie less often than others, and it is possible that overall rates of lying change some over time. But deception will never end. There are too many rewards for lying, and those perks are not just materialistic and they are not just self-centered, either. Most often, the rewards are psychological (rather than, say, financial), and in some (though not most) instances, the person who benefits most from your lies is someone else.

6. The previous five seemingly-dismal pronouncements may actually be good news. Of course, there are domains in which we would love to see perfect lie-detection (in the pursuit of possible murderers, for instance). But perfect lie-detection for every kind of lie in every kind of situation? I think not. Would you really want other people to know – always – how you really do feel, regardless of what you say about how you feel? Would you want them to be able to discern the truth about all of the facts of your life? You can even flip that question: Would *you* want to know what other people really do think of you, all the time and in every situation? Suppose you could magically make all lying disappear: Would you opt to use those special powers? Would you ban the reassuring lies people tell when the truth might be just too painful to bear (e.g., "no, your young daughter did not suffer in that tragic slaying")? Many lies are heinous and cannot be justified in any way. But beware of the urge to find the truth, the whole truth, and nothing but the truth,

always and forever. The cliché, "be careful what you wish for," was written for yearnings such as that one.

2.

Why Do People Lie to You?

8 things about you that tempt others to lie to you

The question of why people lie is profoundly important and endlessly intriguing. Before I turned my attention to research and writing about single people and single life, I spent about two decades studying lying.

When my colleagues and I asked college students and people from the community to keep a diary of all their social interactions and all the lies they told in those social interactions, every day for a week, we were the first to look at lying in such a systematic way. For time immemorial, people had opined about liars and their lies, but without the benefit of careful data on some of the most fundamental questions that might be asked about the matter – questions such as who lies, how often people lie, and why they lie.

Now, there is so much research on lying that a terrific article, "Why We Lie," is the cover story of the most recent issue of *National Geographic.* It takes a lot to wrest my attention away from my singles work these days, but Yudhijit Bhattacharjee's article motivated me to look behind the door of deceit one more time.

For answers to the question of why people lie, look at the *National Geographic* article or some of my earlier work. Here I want to take on a more specific question, rarely addressed in all the other articles and books you can find on lying: Why do people lie TO YOU?

When people lie, sometimes they are doing so because of something about them. I wrote about that in scholarly publications and in a previous article, "Who lies?"

Other times, there is something about YOU that tempts people to lie to you. That's not necessarily a criticism. Sometimes, when people lie to you, it is because of your very best qualities. You are not going to want to change those things – you should continue to be proud of them. But it is useful to know how your strengths can be magnets for other people's lies.

You may have other personal qualities that are not so wonderful that also tempt people to lie to you. Maybe you will want to work on some of those.

I became sensitized to the ways in which we tempt other people to lie to us when my colleagues and I asked 173 people to tell us about the most serious lie they ever told anyone else or the most serious lie anyone ever told to them. You can read some of their stories in *Behind the Door of Deceit: Understanding the Biggest Liars in Our Lives*. Here I will just summarize the key lessons about how we tempt other people to lie to us.

Your Good Qualities that Tempt Other People to Lie to You

#1 *Your high regard and high expectations for the special people in your life*

We all have people in our lives who are special to us. We think highly of them. We are in their corner. That's a wonderful feeling for those people. They know we care about them and expect the best from them.

So what's the problem?

Our high regard is so valuable, they just don't want to disappoint us. When they do something they are not proud of (something all humans do), we are the last person they want to tell. So they lie to us, to maintain our shiny view of them a bit longer.

#2 *Your high moral standards*

Do you have high moral standards? Do you try to do the right thing, even when it is difficult?

That's a good thing.

Maybe your integrity is expressed in your actions, and you never say a word about it. Or maybe you like to talk about your high standards to make them clear to others. Parents sometimes do that when they say things like "we don't lie in this family" or when they express their disapproval of other people's bad behaviors.

The problem, again, is the psychology of disappointment. When other people see you as someone with high moral standards, they don't want to admit to their own failings, not even the small ones we all share. Because you are such a good person, other people are tempted to lie to you when they are not so good themselves.

#3 *Your attractiveness – and not just the physical kind*

We all have qualities that attract other people to us. They might include kindness or generosity or wit or wisdom or empathy or quirkiness or physical attractiveness. Anything that other people like about you is an example of your own personal attractiveness.

So why would your attractiveness tempt other people to lie to you? When other people admire you, they often want to impress you. That might mean lying to you, so they seem more impressive than they really are. They admire you, and that makes them want YOU to admire them. If they don't think you will admire them just the way they are, they will be tempted to lie to you so you will be impressed.

#4 *Your status or power*

Are you someone who has high status or a position of power? Maybe you are someone's boss. Or maybe if you are not the boss, you have some say over whether another person gets a pay raise or a promotion or something else that they want. If you are a teacher, you get to decide your students' grades. Maybe you also write letters of recommendation for them.

You might also have status or power because of what you have accomplished, or who you know.

If you have power over other people, if you have control over their lives, if you have something they want, then they may be tempted to lie to you. Sometimes the lying takes the form of sucking up. They act like you're the greatest person in the world, even if they don't really believe that. Or they try to impress you by lying about their own accomplishments and background. You have a say over what will happen to them in their lives, so they are going to be tempted to say whatever they need to in order to impress you, even if it is a lie.

Your Not-So-Great Qualities that Tempt Other People to Lie to You

Some of the qualities that tempt other people to lie to you are not so great. You may want to work on them. Some of them, though, are not exactly your fault. As I will explain, if you are going through a particularly bad patch, or if you have a personal style that is misinterpreted, you could end up being a magnet for other people's lies.

#5 *You are a scary person*

Some people are scary. Are you one of them? Some people are scary in bad ways and on purpose – bullies, for example. But other people just have a style that can seem intimidating. They aren't trying to be mean or off-putting – it's just the way they are. Do you think you might be like that? If so, that can make it hard for other people to tell you the truth when they are worried that you might not like the truth.

#6 *You are in a bad place, emotionally*

Are you a vulnerable person? Are you easily hurt? Are you depressed? Maybe you are not usually a vulnerable person, but at the moment you are going through a very difficult time.

If you are in a very vulnerable place and other people know that, they may be scared to tell you something you might not want to hear. If they think you can't handle the truth because you are just too fragile, they will be tempted to lie to you.

#7 *You really don't want to know the truth, and other people can tell that about you*

Vulnerable people aren't the only kinds of people who don't want to know the truth. Sometimes very confident and successful people don't want to know either. Powerful CEOs, for example, may make it clear from the way they act that they don't want to hear bad news about their company. When things start to go wrong, the people who could give them a heads-up are afraid to do so. Instead, they suppress vital information or they tell lies.

#8 *You show by example that certain truths should never be spoken*

The way you behave can tell other people whether you want to know the truth, whether you realize it or not. When you can't seem to tell the truth about certain things, you are setting an example for others.

Some parents do this in their interactions with their children, especially when something truly terrible is happening. When a grandparent or other beloved relative or friend is seriously ill, or the cherished family pet is at death's door, parents just don't want to have to tell their kids the awful news.

Parents differ in just how much they protect their kids from painful truths. The ones who do it all the time – even when what they are hiding is not all that awful – are setting an example. They are conveying the message, "We don't talk about difficult things in this family." When their kids grow up, sometimes they act just like their parents did. When something difficult or bad is happening in their lives, they don't tell their parents. They hide that painful reality from their parents, protecting them the way their parents once protected them.

The temptation to try to protect someone from pain – especially someone you love, or someone particularly vulnerable, such as a child – is totally understandable. But what we also need to understand is how even our best instincts can, unwittingly, make us targets for deceit.

II.

Profiles of Ordinary Liars

3.

Who Lies?

What are the personality characteristics of the people who lie the most?

Who lies? My best guess: Everyone.

That's what my research, and others', suggests. For example, in one set of studies my colleagues and I conducted, two groups of people—77 college students and 70 others—kept diaries every day for a week of all of the lies that they told and all of their social interactions lasting at least 10 minutes. The college students lied in one out of about every three of their social interactions; the other people from the community lied in one of every five. Over the course of the week, only 1% of the college students, and 9% of the people from the community, claimed to have told no lies at all. (Yes, my first thought was, *they are lying about not lying.*)

Even though my best guess is that everyone lies, it is clear that some people tell lies more readily than others. In my diary studies, for instance, the lie-telling "champ" told 46 lies over the course of the week—close to 7 a day. Who are these people who lie much more frequently than the rest of us? I'll set aside the clinically diagnosable in this post, and just consider everyday liars. Do they share certain personality characteristics? Are there gender differences? Does age matter? Is the tendency to tell lots of lies linked to the quality of your relationships?

The Personality of a Liar

In the diary studies, all participants filled out a number of personality measures. We used that information to see if certain personality types are especially prone to tell a lot of lies.

When I posed the question, "Who lies?" did a stereotype pop into your mind? Did you guess that frequent liars are more likely to be manipulative and scheming people as well? If you did, I'm not going to tell you to abandon your preconceived notions: People who are more *manipulative* (as measured by a Machiavellianism scale and a measure of Social Adroitness) lie more often than people who are less manipulative.

Manipulative people tend to care about themselves, so you might also think that liars are generally people who do not care about other people. But that's not totally true. Frequent liars can also be people who care *too much* about other people. What they care about, in particular, is what other people think of them. This personality type describes people who are always worrying about the impression they're making on others: *What will she think if I say that? Will he think I'm a total loser if I do this?* This is the *impression-management* personality type, and these people tell lots of lies, too. Interestingly, though, these people *know* that they lie more than others do. That's noteworthy, because like the citizens of Lake Wobegon, the participants in our diary studies believed that, on average, they were *above average* in honesty.

Guess who else lies more? *Extroverts.* Here's where it mattered that we kept track of people's social interactions and not just their lies. If we only counted lies, then extroverts would have many more opportunities to lie than introverts, because they spend more time around other people. So instead, we looked at *rates* of lying—the number of lies people told relative to the number of opportunities they had, and extroverts lied at a higher rate than introverts, although the difference was not substantial.

Why do extroverts tell more lies than introverts? I think it is because the little lies of everyday life can make social interactions run smoothly. Extroverts are versed in social niceties and practice them so often that they probably do not even realize how often they are lying. In fact, we found some evidence for that among the college students. At the end of the week, when the extroverts saw the total number of lies they had told, they said that they were surprised at how often they had lied. (We don't really know for sure, though, why extraverts lie more, so feel free to share your insights.)

The results for one other personality trait are totally obvious: That trait is *responsibility*, as measured by a scale of the same name that identifies people who are responsible, honest, ethical, dependable, and reliable. Responsible people were *less* likely to tell lies than less responsible people—especially the kinds of lies that are self-serving.

Frequent Liars and their Relationships

Participants in the diary studies rated separately the quality of their relationships with people of the same sex as themselves and with people of the other sex. They indicated, for instance, how warm, satisfying, and enduring their relationships tend to be; how much they and their friends understand one another; and the quickness with which they make friends.

People's descriptions of the quality of their relationships with people of the other sex had nothing whatsoever to do with how frequently they lied. It was different for same-sex relationships, though. People who had *higher-quality same-sex relationships* (not just sexual ones) told *fewer* lies overall, and especially fewer self-serving lies, than people with same-sex relationships of lower quality.

Among Adults, Is Age Linked to Frequent Lying?

In our diary studies, we found that the people we recruited from the community told fewer lies than our college students did. Does that mean that older adults tell fewer lies? Not necessarily; our community sample differed in many other ways from our college students. For example, 81% were employed, and 34% had no more than a high school education.

In a separate study, Serota, Levine, and Boster (2010) asked a national sample of adults how often they had lied in the previous 24 hours. They found that as age increased, the number of lies decreased. However, they did not include a measure of opportunities to lie.

We cannot yet say this for sure, but it is likely that over the course of their adult years, people tell fewer lies. Now it is time to follow the same people for years and get them to keep recording their lies the whole time.

Good luck with that!

4.

Men or Women: Who Lies More?

Men and women have different reasons for lying.

How do men and women differ as liars?

In a pair of studies my colleagues and I conducted in the 1990s, two groups of people – college students and people from the community – agreed to keep track of all their social interactions and all of the lies they told during those interactions. They kept these lie diaries every day for a week. The two groups were very different, demographically, but their ways of lying were quite similar.

We calculated each person's rate of lying – the number of lies they told per social interaction.

The most basic question we were able to answer about sex differences was this one: Who lies more often, men or women?

If you guessed women, you are wrong. If you guessed men, you are also wrong. *In the rate at which they tell lies in their everyday lives, men and women are equals.*

Where the real differences show up is in what the men and women are lying about and whom they are trying to fool.

Think about two main reasons for lying:

- **Self-centered** reasons: These are the lies that are all about you. You tell these lies to try to make yourself look better or feel better or protect yourself from embarrassment or disapproval or conflict or from getting your feelings hurt.

- **Kind-hearted** reasons: These are the lies you tell to help or protect someone else. You tell these lies to make someone else look better or feel better, or to protect them from embarrassment or disapproval or conflict or getting their feelings hurt.

People generally tell more self-centered lies than kind-hearted lies. Who tells especially more self-centered lies than kind-hearted lies? Here are your options:

- Men lying to men
- Men lying to women
- Women lying to men
- Women lying to women

The ration of self-serving lies to altruistic lies is especially lopsided when men are talking to other men. Men tell somewhere between three and nine times as many self-centered lies than kind-hearted lies when they are talking to other men.

In only one of the four combinations do people tell just as many kind-hearted lies as self-centered lies. Can you guess which?

It is the last one. When women are lying to other women, they do not tell any more self-centered lies than kind-hearted lies.

Bottom line:

When someone is lying about how fast they ran or how well they performed, it is probably a man talking to another man.

When you hear people saying things they don't mean such as:

- I know just how you feel
- You did the right thing
- You look terrific!
- This is so delicious

you are probably listening to two women. That doesn't mean that women do not value honesty when they are talking with other women. Maybe, though, they value loyalty and their friendship with one another even more. These are the kinds of lies that are intended to be friendly and supportive.

III.

Big-Time Liars

5.

How Ordinary People Become Extraordinary Liars

The trip down Liars Lane

There was a time when I thought I was going to write a book called *How Ordinary People Become Extraordinary Liars*. It never happened. I did, though, write what was going to be the introductory chapter. With the recent revelation that Jonah Lehrer had put words into the mouth of Bob Dylan and published them in his fantastically successful book, *Imagine: How Creativity Works*, I thought it might be the time to share how I frame the issue.

Introduction

"That's my son!" she screamed. She paused a moment, perhaps to catch her breath, or to wonder whether this really could be happening. Then she stood up, cradled her face in her hands, and screamed again.

Out of context, it would have been hard to tell—was her son some big lout who had been exposed on national TV, or had he just won a dazzlingly unexpected and renowned prize?

Turns out, the answer was both. She was Lynne Frey, mother of James Frey, who was the author of the wildly popular memoir of addiction and redemption, *A Million Little Pieces*. The reason she was at the Oprah Winfrey show that autumn day, she thought, was because James knew she loved Oprah and had always dreamed of sitting right there in the audience, so he arranged it. But then the time came for the announcement of the new book club selection. Oprah got no farther than the word *Million* when Lynne Frey began to shout.

Here was the mother of a man who, as Oprah put it, "at 23, has no money, no job, no home and is wanted in three states." And now she was the mother of an author whose memoir was so riveting that it kept Oprah Winfrey up into the wee hours of the night reading it. What a story! I was hooked.

I hadn't been paying much attention to James Frey up to that point. I wasn't even watching the Oprah pronouncement in real time. Instead, I caught the clip on *Larry King Live*. I had heard murmurings that the supposed memoirist had instead been peddling fiction and was just curious enough to turn on the TV while I answered some e-mail.

The accusations were leveled by the website, *The Smoking Gun*. From watching Larry King review the charges and question James Frey about them, I gathered that there were several points of dispute. Did James drive his car up on a curb or hit a policeman with it? Was there a bag of crack in his car at the time, or just a half-consumed bottle of Pabst Blue Ribbon beer? Was he jailed for three months or just held for a few hours, unshackled, until a friend appeared to post a few hundred dollars in bail?

James Frey countered that the disputed section was just eighteen pages of a 432-page book. He had, he said, told the "essential truth", the "emotional truth" about his life, and he stood by it.

His publisher, Doubleday, stood by the book, too. So did his editor, Nan A. Talese; *A Million Little Pieces* was part of her prestigious imprint.

James Frey was trying to calm the tempest, but if his editor and publisher were still issuing claims of support, and his accuser was making the rounds of the television shows, and Larry King was devoting the entire hour to the matter—well, clearly, Frey had not yet succeeded. Larry King was the first

21

to raise the question that everyone seemed to want answered: What did Oprah think? James said he didn't know. Later, a caller got through and asked the question again. Then, Larry King welcomed Lynne Frey to the show and asked her if she expected to hear from Oprah. She didn't know, either.

The show wound down to the last minute, and Larry King asked James for his parting message to his readers. But then the call came in that would extend the broadcast into the next time slot. It was, of course, from Oprah.

It was also everything James and Lynne Frey could have hoped for—a full embrace of James and his message. "Whether or not the car's wheels rolled up on the sidewalk or whether he hit the police officer or didn't hit the police officer is irrelevant to me," Oprah proclaimed. Lynne Frey clapped her hands, child-like, and patted James's hand. Maybe that would be the end of it.

It wasn't.

The wheels of the car and the beer and the policeman and the stint in jail were just the beginning of the liberties that James Frey had taken with his life story. There were fights that never happened, more jail terms that were never imposed, a drug bust that drew the attention of the FBI (only it didn't), and a tragic accident that really did kill two high school girls—but without the role in it that Frey fabricated for himself.

Now I was disgusted. And appalled. And stunned at James Frey's utter stupidity. Did he really think he could make up one outrageous story after another, in a book that millions of readers already had in their hands, and wriggle free of scandal by claiming that, oh, it was just a few pages out of hundreds, and anyway it was the "emotional truth"? What an idiot! I considered myself jaded, and moved on.

By the springtime, I was newly smitten. Stretching across the front page of the books section of my local newspaper was a giant picture of a casually beautiful nineteen-year old, posed against the gate to Harvard Yard. Little, Brown had signed her to a two-book deal of eye-popping proportions—and that was back when she was seventeen, and still in high school. In the meantime, she signed with DreamWorks for the movie deal, and—oh, yeah—while writing the first book, she had also kept up with her first two years of Harvard coursework.

I remember when I was an undergraduate. I took the minimum number of courses, was not writing a novel, and never seemed to have enough time to sleep—and that was without ever pausing to lean on the gates to the campus. I loved Kaavya Viswanathan's story.

There was another author, Megan McCafferty, who had written two books in the same genre, and her fans were not nearly so impressed with Viswanathan as I was. They noticed a number of passages in Viswanathan's just published book, *How Opal Mehta Got Kissed, Got Wild, and Got a Life*, that seemed remarkably similar to sections of McCafferty's books. The *Harvard Crimson* (student newspaper) published the story first, together with thirteen examples of parallel passages.

Within hours, Viswanathan released a statement through her publisher, apologizing to McCafferty and explaining that she had read McCafferty's books a number of times, and that any similarities in wordings "were completely unintentional and unconscious." Little, Brown promised that future printings of the *Opal* novel would be revised to eliminate the similarities. Michael Pietsch, senior vice president of the publishing house, added his strong support: "Kaavya Viswanathan is a decent, serious, and incredibly hard-working writer and student, and I am confident that we will learn that any similarities in phrasings were unintentional."

I was confident, too. It seemed wholly plausible to me that you could read something you liked, reread it a few times, then use the same wording yourself somewhere down the line, without realizing that it was not originally your own. In academic psychology, there is even a term for the phenomenon—"source confusion." I kept my soft spot for Kaavya and her spectacular success story.

Soon a few more parallel passages were uncovered, and a few more after that. At one point, the number was up to forty-five. In short order, *Opal* was pulled from the shelves, the contract for the second book was rescinded, and so were the movie rights.

Viswanathan was finished, and I was left shaking my head still again. Frey and Viswanathan were obviously people with talent, people who could have succeeded without lying, cheating, or plagiarizing. Why did they take the low road when they had other options? And in view of their considerable abilities, how did they let their misrepresentations and misappropriations get so out of hand? Looking back, some of their claims were preposterous, yet smart people swallowed them. Did Oprah really believe that James Frey had a root canal without any anesthetic?

I wanted to know the answers. How do ordinary people become extraordinary liars? I started reading. I researched fraudulent journalists and authors, historians and scientists. I read about grifters and perpetrators of infamous hoaxes. I tracked down books about daring adventurers who only claimed to have accomplished their magnificent feats. I researched medical malingerers, wannabe warriors, and more. I looked for stories from unknown people who wrote about their extraordinary lies, such as the affairs that they pursued for decades. I also read voraciously about big-time deceptions orchestrated by packs of liars, such as the Enron gang and the Watergate guys.

Some of the stories were rollicking tales that were great fun to read. But that's all they were. On the other end of the continuum were riveting reads that included psychological depths and complexities and conflicts in addition to the suspense over whether the deception would succeed.

The latter liars, whose lives read like the stuff of great novels, started out as ordinary people. By that I mean morally ordinary. They engage in bad behaviors and tell serious lies, but they do so with compunction. The first serious lie in a sequence of lies, or the first transgression that tempts the subsequent lies, is unnerving to them. Ideally, they would prefer to be good, decent, and honest people. They worry about the implications of their actions for the well-being of other people (or at least pretend to). They often care a great deal—maybe too much—about what other people think of them. In the beginning of their ill-fated tales, when they take that first step that ultimately leads to a very low and very dark place, they know not where they are headed. What happens to them in the end—what they bring about with their own actions—is not anything that they anticipated or planned.

The other liars are different. To them, their big deceptive adventure is a challenge and a lark. Often, they merrily plan the whole thing in advance. If, in the process, they hurt other people (even people who stood by them all along the way), or if they blemish their profession and create clouds of doubt around those who are practicing their trade with integrity— well, either they just don't think about those things or they don't really care. I think of these people as morally small liars. An example is <u>Clifford Irving</u>, who landed a huge advance to write an "authorized" autobiography of Howard Hughes, a man he never met and knew he never would meet. Irving explained how he felt immediately after he confessed: "I almost wanted to cry out: 'Sure, I did it. And I'm glad I did it. You want me to grovel? I can't. You want me to feel guilty?

I don't. *Because I enjoyed every goddamn minute of it'.*" No conscience, no remorse.

Extraordinary liars are the stars of their own shows, but none of them, no matter how determined, could pull off their infamous deceits without a strong supporting cast. An unending line of adulterers have had assists from the spouse who didn't see what she (or he) was looking at, and the lovers and colleagues who never revealed what they knew. Ben Bradlee and a newsroom full of wise editors at the *Washington Post* signed off on Janet Cooke's Pulitzer-Prize winning story of Jimmy, the eight-year-old heroin addict. It was, of course, fraudulent.

Later, many who were fooled would look back on their experiences with chagrin. Stephen Glass, a reporter who fabricated a whole parade of stories before he was undone, was the topic of a *60 Minutes* piece. During the segment, a litany of Glass's ridiculous lies was recited. Charles Lane, who was executive editor of *The New Republic* during much of the time when Glass was faking his stories, listened, then said, "They were real howlers, weren't they?"

One after another, the editors, colleagues, and friends of Stephen Glass, Janet Cooke, Jayson Blair, and all the others would try to explain, to themselves and to the world, how it was that they got conned. There is a sense of "I still cannot believe this happened" to their accounts. Sometimes, too, there is an unspoken acknowledgment that, despite the countless conversations they've had and the endless hours they have spent ruminating on the matter, they still don't totally understand how the person they thought they knew could have been such a fraud.

The befuddlement is warranted. In the domain of extraordinary lies, the right things work in the wrong ways, and the liars, their lies, and their supporters all get trapped in a tangle of ironies. Consider just a few:

- Intelligence, sensitivity, and the ability to see what lies deep in the hearts of other people can be magnificent talents. But the ordinary people who become extraordinary liars often have just those sorts of skills and use them to give their lies legs.
- When ordinary people are accused of lying, the people in their lives who care about them and believe in them step forward to vouch for them. That's how friends and mentors should act. Ordinarily. But when the accused are actually guilty, those very acts of loyalty can give serious lies a longer life and a safer cover. The liars who may have been mustering the courage to come clean now face another formidable deterrent: Their confession will disappoint and publicly embarrass just those people who tried to stand by them in a time of need.
- When the descent into deceit is in its earliest stages, and just one transgression has been committed or just one lie has been told, is when it is most possible, psychologically and logistically, to step away from the lie. But that is also precisely the time when liars are least inclined to do so.
- Most humans are in the habit of believing. Assuming the truthfulness of others is our default position. Our trusting nature, though, gives an edge to those who would exploit it. And yet, who would choose to reset the human starting point to chronic suspiciousness?

6.

Big-Time Liars: Top 7 Lies They Tell Themselves

The road to deception is paved with self-deception.

For 13 years, Republican presidential candidate Herman Cain maintained what he called a "friendship" with Ginger White, in which he gave her money to pay her bills, and his wife never knew anything about it until now. Ginger White claims that it was an affair; she kept it from her (now grown) children all this time, and only recently had the big talk with them. Newt Gingrich has acknowledged his multiple affairs, and implicitly, all the lies that sustained them.

Big time liars are hardly unique to the political domain. Too close to home (with regard to my professional identity), a social psychologist was recently busted for fabricating a long and seemingly distinguished career's worth of data. There are, of course, the memoirists whose supposed life stories were actually filled with fiction, the plagiarists who make a name on other people's work (until they are caught, whereupon they make a different sort of name for themselves), the fake warriors, the purportedly accomplished athletes who actually cheated and lied their way to victory, and so many more varieties of big-time liars.

The lies that the big-time liars told all of us are intriguing. Perhaps even more fascinating are the lies that they told themselves. What were they thinking?

Over the years, my colleagues and I have collected hundreds of stories about the most serious lies in people's lives. We collected stories from the liars (about the most serious lies they ever told anyone else) and from the targets of the lies - the dupes (about the most serious lies anyone ever told them). After reading transcripts of the stories over and over again, I realized that there were predictable ways that liars fooled themselves about how the process of deceiving another person was going to unfold.

In my book, *Behind the Door of Deceit: Understanding the Biggest Liars in Our Lives*, I discussed each of the most common ways that liars lie to themselves. Here, I will share parts of the discussion of two of the self-deceptions, and list five more. The excerpts are adapted from Chapter 14. You can read the full discussion of all the self-deceptions, as well as the rest of the book, here.

Excerpt from *Behind the Door of Deceit: Understanding the Biggest Liars in Our Lives*:

Thinking of lying? Join the club. Many people who find themselves in a difficult or threatening situation are tempted to try to lie their way out of their troubles. To liars, lies are like wishes. If only their lies really were true, life would be so much kinder, more indulgent, and carefree. And so liars egg themselves on, by telling themselves the following lie myths. I think they are best considered as self-deceptions-- lies that liars tell themselves.

#1. **"I can get away with this lie."**

Few liars embark upon the telling of a serious lie thinking that they are going to get caught. More commonly, they think they can pull it off. My advice to them is, "Don't count on it." Despite their generally high expectations for getting away with their lies, about 40% of the liars in our research were eventually found out.

Liars can develop an inflated view of their chances of success not only because they overestimate their own lie-telling skills, but also because they fail to appreciate the extent to which the fate of their lies is out of their control. If just one other person is in on the lie, if just one other person knows about the lie, or if just one other person knows about the bad behavior that the lie was meant to hide, then all of the lie-telling skills in the world will not save the liar from the risk that the lie will be leaked by that one other person.

Liars usually do realize that the targets of their lies can become suspicious and then try to check out their suspicions. But they are not always fully tuned in to the magnitude of those suspicions or the extensiveness of the target's efforts to learn the truth. Further, some dupes are adept at hiding their suspicions; thus, they can be getting closer and closer to the truth as the liar remains blissfully oblivious. This combination of a clueless liar and a shrewd and sensitive dupe often ends on a shocking note for the liars--they discover all at once that they have been completely undone.

#2. **"No one will ever challenge me - I'll make sure of it."**

#3. **"Even if my lie is discovered, I can make it up to the person I deceived. Eventually, we can have just as good a relationship as we had before."**

#4. **"I have their best interests in mind."**

#5. **"I'm going to confess - later."**

#6. **"This is just between the two of us."**

#7. **"If I can get away with this lie, there will be no costs to telling it."**

Most people who are about to tell a serious lie have no idea just how much *work* it is to maintain the lie. They are obsessively preoccupied with escaping detection, and insistently tell themselves that if only they can forever avoid detection, all will be well. I do not think this is merely self-deception. Rather, would-be liars are often genuinely oblivious to the intensity and the scope of the burdens of concealment. They don't realize how hard it is to protect their serious lie until they've tried.

As long as their lies remain hidden, liars live under the constant threat that someday someone will stumble upon them or dig them up. If the liars live, work, or socialize with people who are most likely to discover the lies, then the liars are stuck doing constant maintenance work to keep their lies well protected and in good repair. They may need to tell lots more lies to cover the first big one, and then, once they do that, they need to do all the work of trying always to remember which particular lies they told to which particular people (and which of those people may have repeated their lies to which other people). This is hard work, it is annoying, and it takes up mental space that most people would far prefer to devote to more comforting thoughts. What's more, it can be a source of great anxiety and stress. Many people who are nurturing a serious lie are living their lives in fear.

Even if their lies are never discovered, many liars still need to deal with their own guilt and shame. (Continued in Behind the Door of Deceit.)

7.

How President Trump's Lies Are Different from Other People's

I thought Trump's lies would be very self-serving; they were, but they were also astonishingly cruel.

My passion is single life, and that's what I most enjoy writing about, but every once in a while, my old interest in the psychology of lying sneaks back into my life. That happened recently, when I saw that reporters at the Washington Post had been keeping a tally of all of Donald Trump's falsehoods, misleading claims, and flip-flops since becoming president.

I had studied the lies of ordinary people years ago. I learned from that research how often people lied, and what kinds of lies they told. I wondered how **Trump**'s ways of **lying** would compare to what my colleagues and I (along with other researchers) had already documented. So I coded the most recent 400 of Trump's lies using the same categories my colleagues and I used when we coded the lies in our research.

I wrote about what I found for the Washington Post. The article generated a lot of interest. It was the most popular article at the Post for a while, and it got picked up by other newspapers and websites in the U.S. and elsewhere. It also attracted 2,000 comments in the first day. That made me think that Psychology Today readers may be interested in hearing more about this, as well as some other observations about Trump's lying that I did not include in my article.

The two most important categories of lies in the studies my colleagues and I conducted were self-serving lies and kind lies. Self-serving lies help liars get what they want and avoid what they don't want, they help liars look better or feel better, or they spare liars from blame or <u>embarrassment</u> or anything else they don't want to experience. Kind lies are the same, only they are told for someone else's benefit. When people lie to help you get what you want, or make you look or feel better, or protect you from something you don't want, they are telling you a kind lie. (You can find some examples of the different kinds of lies in my <u>article</u>.)

Originally, I planned to code Trump's lies into just those two categories. In my previous studies, I found that people tell about twice as many self-serving lies as kind lies. I thought that Trump would tell an even greater proportion of self-serving lies than the people I had studied previously, and that would be the big finding I would get to report.

I was right about Trump telling an especially big proportion of self-serving lies. Instead of telling twice as many self-serving lies as kind lies, he told 6.6 times as many. (His overall rate of lying was higher, too, as I discussed in the <u>article</u>.)

As it turned out, though, that was not the most interesting finding. As I read through Trump's lies in the process of categorizing them, I realized I could not limit myself just to the categories of self-serving and kind lies. I had to add the category of cruel lies — lies that hurt or disparage or embarrass or belittle other people. In the research my colleagues and I did, we found that only 1 or 2 percent of all lies were cruel. That's why I wasn't going to bother with them when coding Trump's lies.

Trump's ways of lying also differed from the previous people I had studied in another way. His lies often served several purposes simultaneously (for example, sometimes they were both self-serving and cruel). In my previous research, it was easy to sort each lie into just one category. (I mention that because it is interesting, and also because it means that, for Trump, the percentages in each category will add up to more than 100 percent.)

Now let me tell you what I found when I tallied Trump's cruel lies. Instead of adding up to 1 or 2 percent, as in my previous research, they accounted for 50 percent. When I first saw that number appear on my screen, I gasped. I knew, of course, that Trump likes to mock and denigrate other people (and countries and agencies), but I didn't realize just how often he was doing that with his lies.

When I first thought about measuring Trump's lies against what my colleagues and I had learned in our previous research, I thought I would look at other psychological processes involved in lying, too. For example, Kathy Bell and I did a series of studies in which we looked at what people did when they were asked about their opinion, but telling the truth about it would hurt another person's feelings.

In those studies, participants were brought into a lab room set up as an art gallery, one at a time. They were asked to choose their favorite and least favorite paintings and write out what they liked and disliked about each one. Only then were they introduced to an art student who, in the key moment of the study, pointed to the participant's least favorite painting and said something like, "That's one of my paintings. What do you think of it?" The participants were also asked about a painting of the artist's that they did like, as well as paintings by another artist they never met.

Participants in the most difficult situation — talking about a painting they hated with the artist who painted it — almost never told the simple truth: "I hated it." Instead, they tried to say things they could defend as truthful, even though what they said was deliberately misleading. For example, they amassed misleading evidence: they often mentioned things they really did like about the painting, while not mentioning as many of the things that they disliked. By describing more aspects that they liked than aspects they disliked, they might give the artist the impression that they liked her painting. Her feelings would not be hurt. And the participants would get to tell themselves (and anyone who challenged them) that, hey, they told the truth — they really did like those things they said they liked.

The participants came up with other interesting strategies, too. For example, they sometimes exaggerated how much they disliked the other artist's work, so that what they said about the work of the artist right there with them would seem more positive in comparison.

Are you starting to realize why I never did similar analyses of Trump's lies? First, the studies Kathy Bell and I did were of kind lies, told to spare the feelings of the artists in our studies. But only about 10 percent of Trump's lies were kind lies (compared to about 25 percent in my previous studies of lying in everyday life).

More importantly, Trump does not seem to care whether he can defend his lies as truthful. Although I cannot know this for sure, he does not appear to feel embarrassment or shame about lying. He doesn't seem to be thinking about how he can lie in ways that can be defended as truthful, as the participants in my previous studies had done. He seems to just state his lies starkly and move on.

In the future, we will know much more about the psychology of Trump's lies. In the brief time since my article was published, several researchers have already contacted me saying that they have studies in progress or articles that have been written but are not yet published.

I originally thought I would title this article, "How Trump Blew Up the Science of Lying," but that is not quite accurate. Trump has not so much defied science as he has nudged social scientists to think in new or more complex or creative ways about <u>how and why people lie</u>.

8.

For Writing about President Trump's Lies, I Got Called an 'Ugly Witch' and More

It seems that more people read my article about Trump's lies than anything else I've ever written. Not all of them liked it.

In the previous article in this book, I offered some background on an article I wrote for the *Washington Post* about President Trump's lies. That article in the *Post* was probably read by more people than anything I have ever written in my life. It was reprinted many places, and in one of them, the Chicago Tribune, it was still appearing now and then in the "most read" section four months later.

Most of the responses were heartening. People wrote thoughtfully about the topic. They asked good questions. I also heard from people in my life I hadn't been in touch with for decades.

However, other readers were incensed. As soon as the article was first published, an army of Trump supporters invaded my email and social media, leaving cruel and hateful messages. On YouTube, for example, someone called me an "ugly witch." On Twitter, someone said, "Its [sic] amazing how many people hate you."

Of course, there was also the predictable hurling of the "libtard" charge, as well as word play using the names of prominent Democrats. I wasn't surprised when one person after another said that if I wanted to study liars, I should look in the mirror.

As this was happening, my home was in the path of the California wildfires. I set up an automatic message on my email account to tell people that I might have to evacuate (I did) and it could take a while for me to get back to them. Two people let me know that they were happy that the wildfires were headed my way. One said, "SOUNDS LIKE GOD'S JUSTICE IS HERE AFTER ALL" and "NOW IS THE TIME TO REPENT." The other proclaimed, "Just maybe we'll get lucky!"

On and on it went. As I stopped for an evening at a friend's house or a motel, I checked my email, only to find still more vitriol amidst the many kind and caring messages from friends and family.

In protest of my article pointing out the extreme level of cruelty in Trump's lies, his supporters sent me extremely cruel emails.

One person tried to harm me in ways that went beyond just name-calling. I'll just say that it wasn't physical, and it wasn't a threat, and leave it at that.

Another line of attack involved expressions of fierce indignation that I had written about the lies of a Republican president but not a Democratic one. Many of those were scathing. They were also ill-informed. I did write about President Clinton's lies and I discussed them on national television shows. Those were different times, of course, but I cannot remember ever getting any vile emails in response.

I know that many other people who have written about Trump have been treated far worse than I have. There was nothing special about what happened to me.

I wonder, though, how many people hold back from saying what they think for fear of such abusive responses. And I wonder how many do say something, but then retreat, because the verbal assault is just too much.

There's something else I wonder about, too. What if all the time and energy and emotions that are now devoted to attacking people were instead channeled into positive and constructive actions that created real social change — change that redounded to the benefit of the people who need it the most?

9.

Deception: It's What Dexter Does Best (Well, Second Best)

Dexter, the affable serial killer, had a way with lying.

Dexter Morgan, man of so little ordinary human sensibility, is an extraordinary liar. What he is covering up with his lies is staggering: Dexter kills people up close and personal. He does it over and over again. Yet hardly anyone ever suspects Dexter's dark heart and even darker deeds.

Dexter's job is in a homicide department; everyone around him is trained and experienced in the pursuit of murderers. Dexter's colleagues, including Dexter's own sister, Debra, work with him every day, but they don't see a killer. Dexter's wife and kids, too, never suspected that Dexter chops people into their component body parts, ties them up in trash bags, and dumps them in the ocean.

How is this possible? How does this person, so baffled by human emotions and so bereft of natural interpersonal talents, walk mostly unchallenged among friends, family, colleagues, and homicide professionals? And what does this tell us about Dexter's real-life cousins-in-crime?

Lying in the Lives of Ordinary Humans

To get a sense of just how often real people lie, my colleagues and I asked 147 people (including college students and a diverse group of people from the community) to keep a record of all of the lies that they told, and all of their social interactions, every day for a week. Over the course of the week, the participants told about one or two lies a day, which amounted to about one lie in every four social interactions. Only seven people claimed never to have lied at all. (Maybe if our study lasted longer, even they would have 'fessed up to telling some lies.)

Most of the lies the participants recorded were little lies. For example, they lied about:

- Their *feelings and opinions* ("I told him I missed him and thought about him all the time when I really don't think about him at all;" "I told her that she looked good when she really looked like a blimp")
- Their *actions, plans, and whereabouts* ("Lied about where I had been; didn't tell them all of the places;" "Said I sent the check this morning")
- Their *achievements and failings* ("Led him to believe I had been a daring ski jumper;" "Tried to appear knowledgeable about operating room procedures when I only knew a little about them")
- Their *reasons and explanations* ("I told everyone at work I was late because I had car trouble;" "I told him I didn't take out our garbage because I didn't know where to take it.")

There were some big lies scrawled in participants' lie diaries, but not enough to satisfy our perverse interest. So in the next set of studies, we asked people to tell us specifically about the most serious lie they ever told and the most serious lie anyone ever told to them. In response, we heard much taller tales and stories of much more consequential transgressions, though no one confessed to murder. We learned about many adulterers, about people who lied about the severity of an illness (their own or someone else's), some who lied to almost everyone around them about their sexual identity, and much more.

The stereotype we have of liars is that they are crass, materialistic, exploitative, and uncaring about other people. They want something – such as a better grade, a better job, money, or sex – and they will lie to get it. Although liars like that do exist, after studying thousands of lies, big and small, one thing became very clear to me: Lies told merely to fulfill immediate crass desires are the exceptions.

Instead, ordinary humans usually tell lies because they care. They care about what other people think of them. They *want* other people to think they are a daring ski jumper and not a couch potato. They don't want others to know that they were late for work because they are so disorganized that they couldn't get out the door on time. They don't want a potential employer to realize how little they actually know – not just because that would undermine their chances of getting the job, but also because they might come across as the kind of person who would put a patient at risk just to get hired. That hit to their reputation would hurt.

Ordinary people also lie because they care about other people's feelings and reputations. If that college student had told her boyfriend the truth about how she really felt about him – that she never even thinks about him – he would have been devastated. Even though she is not attracted to him, she doesn't want to wound him. People who lie about the seriousness of their own illness or that of a beloved relative or friend are often trying to spare others from worry. It would be hard to argue that adulterers are not trying to satisfy their own needs and desires – and I'm not going to try. Sometimes, though, there is more at stake than the opportunity to continue their romps undeterred. Telling the truth about their transgressions would ruin their reputation and hurt the person who should have been the sole recipient of their intimacies. Some adulterers actually do care about both.

Dexter lies about some of the same kinds of things that the rest of us do. For example, he tells many lies about his actions, plans, and whereabouts, about what he knows and doesn't know, and why he does some things and not others. His underlying motives, though, are simpler. Ultimately, all of his lies are told in the service of one goal – hiding who he really is and what he really does, so he can continue to do it. At times Dexter pretends to care about how other people feel and what they think of his skills and his character, but that's only because he *has to* fake all that to get away with his killing. Psychologically, that puts Dexter on a whole different planet from Deb, Rita, LaGuerta, Angel, Masuka and you and me. As non-psychopathic humans, we almost can't help but care what others think of us.

The *Dexter Morgan Show*: The Writer/Director Tries to Make It Unremarkable

Dexter is the writer, producer, star cast member, and director of *The Dexter Morgan Show*. Like *The Truman Show*, it is a program that (almost) never goes off the air. Unlike every other person in show business, though, Dexter wants his performance to be utterly unremarkable. He wants viewers to turn away in boredom -- nothing to see here. That's because the first step in getting away with a lie is to make sure that the question of whether or not you *might* be lying never even comes up.

The extraordinary Dexter Morgan works at trying to appear utterly ordinary. He doesn't say much and, as a guy, can get away with seeming like the stereotypical unemotional and unexpressive type. His clothes are uninteresting and so is his hair style (if you can call it that).

Appearing low-key and staying in the background is useful to Dexter because he has so little intuitive sense of what to say or how to act. There's a risk to too much of that, though – he could start seeming like the "loner" who "keeps to himself." That would be trouble! So Dexter does what he can to seem like one of the gang. He's the donut guy. That's easy enough – bring donuts, make people think you're a nice, thoughtful person. He goes out with the guys, knowing he's not going to have a good time. He let his friends throw him a bachelor party and pretended to enjoy it, all the while wishing he could just go out and kill someone.

Perhaps the best props in Dexter's show are Rita and the kids. How ordinary does that seem? The irony is that having a spouse or kids is actually *not* a great indicator of whether you might be a serial killer. In their book *Homicide: A Sourcebook of Social Research*, criminologists John Fox and Jack Levin note that many serial murderers "hold full-time jobs, are married or involved in some other stable relationship, and are members of various local community groups." What Dexter realizes, though, is that it is the conventional wisdom that counts. If other people generally believe that serial killers are loners and that men in families would rarely do any harm, then the family man is the role to play.

What Makes Dexter Such an Extraordinarily Successful Liar?

To find out what makes Dexter such a great liar, we can start by looking inside him. That's what we'll do in this section. To get away with a life of lies, Dexter benefits from what he does have – his smarts – and perhaps even more interestingly, from what he doesn't have – deep emotions and a conscience. Let's start with the have-nots.

No Emotions? No Problem

When ordinary people lie to someone face-to-face about where they were the night before or how their car got smashed, they risk being betrayed by their own feelings. If they are worried about getting caught in their lie, if they feel guilty about what they did wrong or about the fact that they are telling a lie, they might come across differently than they would if they were telling the truth and not experiencing any of those emotions. Liars sometimes seem more tense than truth-tellers, and they can sound like they don't really want to commit to what they are saying. Those kinds of differences in demeanor can tip off a listener that something is amiss.

Dexter, though, is emotionally stunted. He just doesn't understand human feelings. He doesn't often have them, and he usually doesn't know how to deal with other people's emotions.

When it comes to getting away with lies, emotional emptiness is not such a bad thing. That guilt that other people feel about their lies that can show in their behavior and give them away? Dexter doesn't have that. The apprehensiveness about getting caught that can reveal itself in a nervous demeanor? Sure, Dexter is bound and determined to get away with his lies, but he doesn't experience much anxiety about the matter.

Dexter typically thinks of Harry's code as a way to avoid getting caught. By season four, though, he realizes that the code also helps shield him from experiencing emotions.

Where Dexter runs into trouble as a plausible liar is when he has to fake emotions. The appropriate feelings don't come naturally to Dex, and sometimes he just forgets that he's supposed to be feeling something and needs to pretend. That's one of the mistakes Dexter made that set off Sergeant Doakes's suspicions. After Angel was stabbed, his concerned friends and colleagues were at his side at the hospital. When word came that Angel would survive, everyone was visibly relieved. Well, everyone but Dexter. Doakes noticed.

Like an anthropologist trying to discern the ways of an unfamiliar tribe, Dexter studies his fellow humans for cues to how to behave. After Dexter's first two stunningly unromantic marriage proposals to Rita were rebuffed, he knew he couldn't figure out this sentimentality thing on his own. Luckily, he heard someone else wax poetic about true love (never mind that the woman was a delusional murderer!). Then he came home to Rita and says the same thing in the same way. Proposal accepted.

No Conscience? No Problem

When Robert Hare, one of the world's foremost authorities on psychopaths, wrote a book about them, he called it *Without Conscience*. That lack of conscience is probably the quality that most starkly separates psychopaths such as Dexter from everyone else. In fact, it may be Dexter's inability to experience the ordinary range and depth of emotions – especially feelings such as fear and anxiety – that accounts for his failure to develop a conscience.

Dexter, though, has a serviceable substitute – Harry's code. Dexter's foster father realized that Dexter's urges to kill would be uncontrollable, so he channeled and regulated them instead. Dexter is only allowed to kill people who deserve it. He can't get caught. Those are the two most important rules in the Code of Harry. The whole set of rules functions as a moral checklist. Dexter doesn't have to have an inner guiding light; he can just go down the list.

If it is your goal to kill people, lie about it, and get away with the wicked deed and the lie, then not having a conscience, like not having emotions, is not such a bad thing. If you are an ordinary, morally grounded human who is tempted to transgress, your sense of right and wrong can give you pause. That feeling that you are about to do a bad thing is like a moral stomach ache; it warns you that you had better stop indulging if you want to feel good again. Not so for Dexter. His has a stomach of steel. He will lie and manipulate and destroy evidence to stay in the clear, without even a twinge or guilt or shame. And if others, despite Dexter's best efforts, become suspicious anyway, well, let's just say that Dexter may just take matters into his own hands.

Dexter's No Dummy

Watch Dexter as he sizes up a blood-drenched scene and in an instant deduces the entire choreography of the criminal and the crime. Listen to his repartee with his fellow serial killer who was a used-car salesman. The salesperson tossed out one lie after another, and Dexter batted each one away without missing a beat. Notice how Dexter observes other people and commits their words and intonations to memory. Remember when Dexter was young and Harry told him how to come across as normal on a mental health assessment? Dexter nailed it.

All lines of evidence lead to the same conclusion: Dexter is no dummy. His smarts help him get away with both his crimes and his lies. While other liars might stumble around as they try to fabricate the perfect lie and struggle to remember what they already said and to whom – making it all the more obvious that they have something to hide – Dexter thinks quickly and sharply. The mental challenges of telling lies don't trip him up.

The significance of a good memory became especially apparent when Dexter suffered a concussion after his car accident in season four. Suddenly, he can't remember what he did with Benny Gomez's remains. How un-Dexter-like!

Dexter's cautiousness is smart, too. His trophy blood slides are so well hidden that only someone as determined as Doakes, who was willing to tear Dexter's place apart, would ever find them. His office is in good shape, too. When the feds descended upon Miami Homicide to help with a particularly daunting case, Dexter gave them the password to his computer and walked away. He knew they weren't going to find anything.

A friend and colleague of mine, Weylin Sternglanz, had a great idea for his doctoral dissertation when he was a student in my lab. He thought that people trying to get away with their lies would be more successful if they admitted to a lesser offense than if they simply tried to deny that they had done anything wrong. It worked for Dexter – twice. Once, when Rita was becoming suspicious that something was amiss and asked whether Dexter was an addict, he said that he was. That answer satisfied her, especially after Dexter committed to going to the twelve-step meetings. Later, Doakes began tailing Dexter, certain that he would discover him doing something horrible. When instead his chase led him to the basement meeting of a Narcotics Anonymous group, Doakes thought all the pieces had fallen into place. Dexter wasn't avoiding him and acting suspicious because he was out committing crimes; he was just hiding his personal problem and the work he was doing to deal with it.

Rita, Deb, and All His Colleagues and Friends: Dexter's Unwitting Enablers

Having people around all the time can be quite an impediment, even to the determined liar. They see too much and know too much. Dexter had good reason to want his own space. Who wants some nice person around who, when the air conditioner breaks, might pull it out of the wall and try to fix it? Or who might wonder why you are getting home so late? Dexter lied to Rita about keeping his apartment because there, the Dark Defender could plot his evil deeds unmonitored and undeterred.

In other ways, though, the important people in Dexter's life enable his lies. They don't mean to, but they do. First, the mere presence of friends, a (now former) partner, kids, and a sibling he sees all the time shield Dexter from suspicion. They make him seem normal.

The second reason is perhaps not what you would think. Ask people if they can tell when someone close to them is lying, and often they will claim some special insight that strangers do not have. They'll say something like, "Oh, yeah, I can always tell when he's lying." And why shouldn't they? They have so much more experience observing, reading, and interacting with their close relationship partners than acquaintances or strangers do. And yet, when put to the test, romantic partners in particular are not very good at knowing when their loved one is lying and when they are telling the truth. The problem is they *want* to believe that their partners would never lie – especially not to them. As a result, they see their partners as telling the truth more often than they should, and more often than a stranger would.

Here's a clever example of a study that demonstrates romantic partners' obliviousness to one another's deceit. It was conducted by Eric Anderson, for his dissertation, when he was a graduate student in my lab.

Anderson's study modeled the dreaded question asked of one partner to the other, while pointing out a nearby stranger: "Do you think that person is attractive?" In the experiment, the person who was put on the spot – let's use the name Bernie since it could apply to a man or a woman – answered truthfully half the time and lied the other half. Their romantic partners of all the different Bernies were just a shade better than chance at knowing when the answers were lies. (They were right 52 percent of the time, when they would have gotten 50 percent right simply by guessing.)

Each of the 100 couples was joined by a stranger who also tried to determine whether Bernie was lying. The strangers were not very good at detecting deception either, but at 58 percent, they were better than the partners.

Anderson, though, did not stop at asking the participants directly whether they thought that the person in question was lying or telling the truth. He also asked them some indirect questions, such as how confident they were about each answer, whether they had gotten enough information to make an accurate judgment, and whether they felt at all suspicious. When the romantically involved participants said that they were not very confident, that they needed more information, and that they felt a bit suspicious, their partner was more likely to be lying than to be telling the truth. So even though the sweethearts were hardly better than chance when they were asked directly whether their partners were lying, they did seem to know, at some level, that something was not quite right. Interestingly, the strangers did not show as much sensitivity to the more subtle signs that something was amiss.

As the people around Dexter observe his behavior, we would probably expect Rita (were she still alive) to be the first to notice when something seemed not quite right. Part of the tension and drama in the developing relationship between the two came from Rita's growing sense of unease about what was really going on with Dexter. Yet, Rita might also be the last to conclude that Dexter was lying. Give her something else to hang her suspicions on – oh, he's using! – and she'll grab it.

Deb, of course, is close to Dexter, too. Maybe she also has a deepening sense of foreboding about the brother who is so important to her. But she is no more eager than Rita was to add up all the clues and label Dexter a monstrous liar.

Dexter's Cousins in Crime

In real life, there are there people like Dexter who kill repeatedly over many years, yet live unsuspected among family and community. The BTK killer was one of them. BTK is the name that Dennis Rader gave himself because he bound, tortured, and killed his victims. He was married with two children and active in his church. He murdered ten people but was not caught until thirty-one years after his first kill. John Wayne Gacy was another. He was a married man who murdered thirty-three men and entombed many of them under the crawl space of his home. His wife remained clueless.

These and other psychopathic killers are Dexter's cousins in crime. So are some other big-time miscreants who pile lie upon lie in the service of other horrible deeds – for example, perpetrators of massive Ponzi schemes that leave hundreds destitute and humiliated. What makes these people Dexter's blood relatives (so to speak) is not so much the nature of their deeds as the character of their feelings about their crimes. They don't feel bad about them.

Some even bask in the joy of their deceptive triumphs. An example is Clifford Irving, who landed a huge advance to write an "authorized" autobiography of Howard Hughes, a man he'd never met and knew he never would meet. Irving explained how he felt immediately after he confessed: "I almost wanted to cry out: 'Sure, I did it. And I'm glad I did it. You want me to grovel? I can't. You want me to feel guilty? I don't. *Because I enjoyed every goddamn minute of it.*'" No conscience, no remorse.

Ordinary people who do have a conscience can still become big-time liars, but for them the experience is much different. Every step they take into the muddy moral quagmire of cheating and deceiving threatens to sink them ever more deeply into guilt and shame. They end up feeling dirty – and physically ill. John Dean, White House counsel to President Richard Nixon from 1970 to 1973, was a key player in the infamous Watergate scandal, but not a very happy one. His fellow perpetrators were sometimes exasperated by his moral misgivings. Ultimately, Dean would star in an iconic moment in American history when he exposed the "cancer on the Presidency" during the Watergate hearings.

Dean described how he felt when the cover-up was in its last throes, but just before he had decided to tell the truth. His account could hardly be more different from Clifford

Irving's: "My thoughts, I realized, were no longer measured or rational. Every breath I drew in seemed cold, and the chill latched on to my thoughts and dragged them down into my stomach, then around up my spine. My cool, my detached calculation, was dissolving in fear."

Offenders without a conscience are the most dangerous criminals because only we can stop them. Culprits such as John Dean who do feel remorse will sometimes stop themselves.

So am I tossing Dexter into the bin with the worst of the worst? Maybe not. Dexter is not a hardcore unwavering psychopath. He has grown over the course of the series. He's started to feel something akin to real fondness and concern for other people. He's begun to worry that – should he ever get caught – his undoing would be devastating to other people, too, and not just to him. All those emotions make Dexter more human. But they also threaten to make him a less effective liar. Ironically, then, Dexter's growing humanity may be his undoing.

Alternatively, maybe Dexter's newfound feelings for other people will motivate him to stop killing. Perhaps he *will* stop himself. Then he won't need to lie so much. With Dexter (and his brilliant writers), you just never know what's going to happen next.

[This essay originally appeared in The Psychology of Dexter, *edited by Bella DePaulo, PhD, with Leah Wilson. The book was published in 2010 by Smart Pop, an imprint of BenBella Books, Dallas, Texas.]*

10.

Getting Suckered by a Killer

Don't blame police officers for believing the lies of people who go on to become murderers.

How many people must that mass murderer have fooled about who he was and what he was about to do before he went on a rampage and killed six people and injured many more? It happened just outside of the campus of University of California at Santa Barbara, the university I've been associated with for nearly 14 years.

I have to admit that when I heard that law enforcement personnel (four sheriff's deputies, a police officer, and a dispatcher) had been <u>sent to talk to the killer</u> less than a month before his killing spree, my jaw dropped. The killer's mother and therapist had both become disturbed by the videos he had been posting and contacted the police to ask them to check up on him.

The deputies talked to him outside his apartment, and he reassured them that it was all a misunderstanding. They never went inside; if they had, they may have discovered a frightening cache of guns and ammunition. After they left, the officers described the soon-to-be-killer as "shy, timid, and polite."

I'm here today to defend those deputies and officers who talked to the killer on that fateful night. I'm not defending their decision not to go inside, or not to look at the online videos. Whether they acted within the bounds of the current rules and procedures on those matters is for others to figure out.

What I am defending is the fact that, after a brief interaction with the person who was planning a mass murder, they walked away not the least bit suspicious of the person. He was lying, and they totally and completely failed to detect his lies.

Before I started studying of single life, I spend decades doing research on the psychology of lying and detecting lies. My colleagues and I reviewed every study ever conducted on people's accuracy at detecting deception, and we found that people are amazingly <u>unimpressive at knowing when other people are lying</u> and when they are telling the truth, based just on what they say and how they say it (their verbal and nonverbal behavior). On the average, in situations in which people would get 50% right just by guessing, they typically get just 54% right.

Some have claimed that people in jobs that involve the detection of deception, such as police officers, are better at detecting deception than ordinary people. A colleague and I tested that possibility in a study of federal law enforcement officers, from those just starting out to advanced officers. The officers, including the advanced ones, were no better at detecting deception than the college students – they just thought they were. They had greater confidence, but no greater accuracy.

In many other studies, too, people in deception-relevant jobs are generally no better at detecting deception than people without such job-related experiences. Occasionally there is a study suggesting that people in a particular group are a bit better than others, but then the replication studies are not done or do not support the original findings.

Another question is whether you could train people, such as sheriff's deputies, to be able to detect deception. Many attempts to train people to detect deception better have produced discouraging results. Some people, such as Paul

Ekman, claim to be able to train people to detect deception at high levels of accuracy, but Ekman has never published any training studies so fellow scholars are unable to look closely at his work. A few studies here and there suggest one-time successes at improving deception-detection accuracy by training methods. Those studies need to be replicated, and then we need to know whether the accuracy at the types of lies and kinds of situations used in the training would generalize to, say, a group of sheriff's deputies having a brief conversation with a college student outside of his apartment.

My bottom line: Don't blame those officers for not knowing that the would-be killer was lying to them, just from talking to him for a short time. Hardly anyone is good at that, whether they are professionals in jobs that involve lie-detection on a day to day basis, whether they have gotten training, or whether they are just ordinary people. Lie-detection is hard in those situations, and fooling people is easy.

IV.

Figuring Out When You Are Getting Duped

11.

Looks Can Kill – Your Better Judgment

An angelic look can fool government agents.

Who can we believe? The recent debacle of the discredited accuser in the Dominique Strauss-Kahn case has put the issue of credibility front and center of our national (and international) discourse. There is a science of credibility. It is part of the research on the psychology of deceiving and detecting deceit, which was my primarily scholarly preoccupation before I pointed my passions to the study of singles.

A remarkable series of studies was just published in the most recent issue of *Human Communication Research*. The studies, by Tim Levine and his colleagues, document the power of one particular factor - a person's looks (demeanor) - on other people's judgments of whether or not that person is lying.

There are people who just look honest and trustworthy - both when they really are communicating honestly and deserve to be believed, and when they are lying. Then there are the more unfortunate types who just chronically look dishonest - both when they are lying and deserve to be disbelieved, and when they are telling the truth. That's what I mean by "looks" in this post. The authors call it "demeanor."

Maybe you have heard the claim that there are some people who are superb lie-detectors. The TV show *Lie to Me* features a lead character based on the scholar, Paul Ekman, who makes that claim most insistently. Not everyone accepts that claim uncritically, as Charles Bond and I detailed in this collection. (A few other relevant books are here.)

To be a great lie-detector, it is not enough to know a lie when you see (or hear or read) one. You also need to recognize a truthful statement. Skillful human lie-detectors can distinguish truths from lies.

Skillful lie-detectors should not be fooled by a person's looks. They should be able to see beyond a person's characteristic angelic or devilish look to discern when each person really is lying and whey they are really telling the truth. But can people do this? Suppose people without any special training or experience in the detection of deception get fooled by a person's looks. Will the same be true of people who work at national security-related jobs and who have had formal training?

When a person's characteristic look matches their actual truthfulness, the task of figuring out whether they are lying should be a (relatively) easy one. Sincere-looking people telling the truth represent one kind of match: both their look and their actual truthfulness suggest that they are telling the truth. The other kind of match occurs when insincere-looking people are lying. If you go by their characteristic look, you will think they are lying, and if you can recognize cues to deception, you will also know that they are lying.

The more challenging cases are the mismatches: sincere-looking people who are lying, and insincere-looking people who are telling the truth.

Levine had a collection of videotapes from more than 100 American college students who had an opportunity to cheat while playing a trivia game. Those who did well at the game could win a cash prize, so it was tempting to cheat. Plus, there was a fellow student egging them on (a confederate, actually, but the students didn't know that). Some took the bait and cheated - then lied about it when interviewed later. Others resisted the temptation and told the truth when interviewed.

The videotapes of all of the lying cheaters, and a comparable group of non-cheating truth-tellers, were judged by 64 undergraduates, who guessed whether each person on the tape was lying or telling the truth. From those judgments, Levine could determine who was most often believed and who was most often disbelieved. From all of the videotapes, he chose 20 to use in the key studies I'll describe below.

The Matches

- 5 truth-tellers who were very often judged to be telling the truth (they were sincere-looking)
- 5 liars who were very often judged to be lying (they were insincere-looking)

The Mismatches

- 5 truth-tellers who were very often judged to be lying (they were insincere-looking)
- 5 liars who were very often judged to be telling the truth (they were sincere-looking)

The researchers showed the 20 video clips to five different groups: two groups of American college students, one group of Korean college students, a group of university professors (perhaps they have experience with students who may have cheated), and a group of government agents from a security and intelligence agency. The agents had a range of experience at the job, and they all had training in deception-detection.

In the first column of the table below are the accuracy scores of all 5 groups at the easy task: judging the truthfulness of the people whose "look" matched their actual truthfulness. Everyone did well at that. Even the Korean college students, who were judging English-speakers even though English was not their native language, got 71% of the matched examples right. And look at those government agents - when a person's "look" and their actual truthfulness pointed in the same direction, the agents' accuracy at guessing their actual truthfulness was 96%!

% Accuracy (averaged across truths and lies)

Match	Mismatch	Who made the judgments?
79	36	U.S. college students
78	41	More U.S. college students
71	34	Korean college students
78	41	University professors
96	34	US government agents

But now look at the second column (above). When faced with the challenging task of judging mismatches, every group did poorly. In fact, they did worse than chance! Because half of the people on the tapes were lying and half were telling the truth, a person could get a score of 50% just by guessing. Instead, people in all five groups were more likely to be influenced by a person's "look" than by their actual truthfulness, when those two elements clashed.

I've saved the most powerful results for last. It turned out that about half of the agents had fewer than eight years of experience, and the others had more than 14 years of on-the-job experience. That's a big difference. So was it the less experienced agents who were pulling down the scores of the entire group?

The next table (below) shows the results of the less experienced and the more experienced agents. First let's look at the matches. The more experienced intelligence and security agents literally cannot be beat. If they are judging the truthfulness of sincere-looking people who really are telling the truth, or insincere-looking people who are lying, they are correct every single time. The less experienced agents are not far behind.

Now look at their accuracy at judging the truthfulness of the mismatches. Across all of the mismatches, both groups of agents are terrible - the less experienced get only 37% correct, and the more experienced agents do even worse, at 20%.

Finally, look at the very last row. The people on the tapes really are lying, even though they are characteristically sincere-looking people. Accurate judges of deception would see beyond their angelic looks and call them liars. The most experienced government agents did the worst at this task. They were correct only 14% of the time. That means that 86% of the time, they were fooled by the liars who have a sincere manner about them, and judged those liars to be telling the truth.

% Accuracy

| 95 | 100 | ALL MATCHES |

Specific matches

| 93 | 100 | Telling truth, sincere-looking |
| 97 | 100 | Lying, insincere demeanor |

| 37 | 20 | ALL MISMATCHES |

Specific mismatches

| 54 | 36 | Telling truth, insincere-looking |
| 30 | 14 | Lying, sincere-looking |

[In the table above, the *first number* in each row is the percent accuracy for government agents with *less experience* and the *second number* is the percent accuracy for government agents with *more experience*. The text describes what they are judging – for example, sincere-looking people who are telling the truth.]

12.

Why Are We So Bad at Detecting Lies?

Surprise! We're not using the wrong cues.

People are pretty lousy lie detectors. In ordinary social interactions, when all we have to go by is what the other persons are saying and how they are saying it, our judgments of whether someone is lying or telling the truth are correct only a little more often than chance. My colleague Charlie Bond and I discovered that when we summarized the results of all of the studies that had ever been done on the topic, in which more than 24,000 people had participated. By chance, accuracy would have been 50 percent; the average accuracy across all the studies was 54 percent.

Peruse any popular website that features social science research and sooner or later you will come across an article or blog post with a title such as "How to tell when someone is lying." You can find those articles in scholarly journals, too. I've written some myself, including a massive review. (The version laden with jargon and statistics is here; the readable version is here.)

Often, when people promise to tell you about cues to deception, what they are implying is that you aren't that great at detecting lies because you don't know what to look for. You don't know how people really do behave differently when they are lying compared to when they are telling the truth.

But is that really true?

If you ask people directly to tell you how they know when people are lying, they will often give you answers that are way off base. For example, they seem sure that liars won't look you in the eye, or that they fidget a lot, when research shows that those behaviors are not very useful indicators of whether a person is lying.

There is a better way to know what behaviors people see as relevant to deception, and that's to look at the cues they rely on when they make actual judgments of whether a person is lying or telling the truth. In the typical study, people watch a video of people who are lying or telling the truth, and they record their judgments of the truthfulness of each person on the video. Researchers can then correlate the behaviors of the persons on the video with the judgments of the viewers. For example, when people on the video smile a lot, are they more or less likely to be judged as lying?

Such studies tell us which behaviors are *judged* to be indicative of deception, not which behaviors really are cues to deception. In a comprehensive review article, Hartwig and Bond found a number of cues that are important to people's judgments of deceptiveness.

People Will Think You Are Lying If You...

#1

...tell stories that are not very compelling. If you tell stories that do not sound plausible or logical, people will probably think you are lying. If you don't seem very involved in what you are saying, if you are not very direct, same thing – you are likely to be judged as deceptive. Coming across as ambivalent or indifferent or uncertain is also a credibility-killer.

#2

...seem less than forthcoming. If you are stingy with details, or if you refuse to discuss certain topics, don't be surprised if people think you might have something to hide.

#3

...*seem tense*. People who seem nervous are generally less likely to be believed than people who do not seem tense.

#4

...*are not very positive or pleasant*. If you are unfriendly or uncooperative or if you have an unpleasant facial expression, you are stacking the deck against your own credibility. People are less likely to believe you. On the other hand, if you have a baby face, or if you seem competent, people are more likely to believe that you are telling the truth.

Are the Cues People Are Using the Cues They *Should* Be Using?

The cues people should use to judge deceptiveness are the ones that really do separate the liars from the truth-tellers. Hartwig and Bond (2011) looked at results for more than 50 cues and found that for about two-thirds of them, people *were* using the cues they should have been using. When there were discrepancies, people were relying on particular cues more than they should have been. For example, people's faces really do look a little less pleasant when they are lying than when they are telling the truth, but those who are making judgments about deceptiveness think that facial pleasantness matters more than it really does.

What never happened is that people, on the average, were using cues the wrong way. They might make too much of an unfriendly person, but they don't head down the exact wrong track by thinking that people acting friendly are significantly more likely to be lying than people acting unfriendly. They get it that it's the unfriendly faces that are, on the average, less likely to be trustworthy.

It is also possible to look at the overall pattern of the cues that people used in their deception judgments and compare that to the pattern of cues that people should be using. Again, those analyses showed that people are generally using the right cues. The correlation between the two sets of cues is at least .59. That's not a perfect relationship but it is pretty good.

If People Are Using the Right Cues, Why Aren't They Better Lie-Detectors?

Cues to deception are not that useful. There are ways that people act differently when they are lying than when they are telling the truth (that's what a cue to deception is), but the differences are not all that big or reliable. So, for example, on the average, liars seem more nervous than truth-tellers. But the difference is unimpressive in its size. And, there are lots of exceptions. Sometimes liars do not seem particularly nervous. Also, people can be nervous for reasons that have nothing to do with whether they are lying or telling the truth. Maybe they are worried about being disbelieved. Or maybe they are stressing about something else entirely.

If you want to know whether someone is lying, you can't just sit back and observe their verbal and nonverbal behaviors. If you are a detective, you may need to learn how to ask the kinds of questions that trip up liars, getting them to reveal more than they should. Or you just need to go out and find more reliable evidence.

Reference:

Hartwig, M., & Bond, C. F. Jr. (2011). Why do lie-catchers fail? A lens model meta-analysis of human lie judgments. *Psychological Bulletin, 137,* 643-659.

13.

How Body Language Lets Us Down

Think you can tell when someone's lying? Think again.

We love to believe that we can figure out what other people are thinking and feeling without needing to hear a word they say. Those tell-tale eyes that are windows to the soul, that posture that's a little off, the ever-so-slightly downturned mouth—don't they all tell us volumes? And if we do listen to words, isn't the tone just as telling as the content?

Before I became so passionate about the study (and not just the practice) of single life, my area of expertise was the psychology of deceiving and detecting deceit. I even taught a course in nonverbal communication for many years. I know that the idea that nonverbal cues are linked to thoughts and feelings is not entirely bogus—there really can be something there.

The problem is, there's often far less there than we believe.

It is not just ordinary humans who want to believe in the power of body language. The *New York Times* just posted John Tierney's article, "At airports, a misplaced faith in body language." Tierney notes that the federal government poured about $1 billion into training airport personnel to tell if you might be a terrorist just by looking at your nonverbal behaviors as you stand in line waiting to get screened. (I discussed the program here previously.)

The problem with relying on nonverbal behaviors as clues to deception (or as clues to feelings and emotions) is that they are not very strong or very reliable. The always-insightful

Maria Hartwig, referring specifically to our pet theories about deception, says that it is a "little more than a cultural fiction" that "liars betray themselves through body language."

Nicholas Epley, author of *Mindwise: How We Understand What Others Think, Believe, Feel, and Want*, put it beautifully when he told Tierney, "Body language speaks to us, but only in whispers."

In the *Times* article, Tierney discusses the review article I wrote with Charlie Bond, in which we analyzed the deception-detection accuracy of more than 24,000 people who participated in more than 200 studies. The results were bad news for those who would put their faith in humans as lie detectors. On average, people were only correct about determining when people were lying 54 percent of the time. (They'd have been right 50 percent of the time just by guessing.) Ouch.

The impotence of particular clues to deception became glaringly evident when my colleagues and I conducted a similarly comprehensive review of every study ever conducted on particular nonverbal behaviors and whether they might provide evidence that a person is (or is not) lying. In "Cues to Deception," we did find some cues, but there were very few relative to the number of behaviors we examined, and even those we did find were weak or inconsistent.

Our papers are academic reports, and people reading them who have not spent years in graduate work in the social sciences may not realize something—the results were even more disappointing than they seemed. Consider: When we found that a particular behavior was statistically linked to lying—for example, that liars seem more nervous than truth-tellers—we said that nervousness was a cue to deception. And it was. Across all the studies that measured nervousness, liars, *on average*, appeared more nervous than truth-tellers. But here's the catch: Not all people appear more nervous when they are lying than when they are telling the truth. And not all studies showed that liars appeared more nervous than truth-tellers. The same sobering qualifications are true of other nonverbal cues to deception.

There's another important way that nonverbal clues let us down: We are unimpressive judges of what our *own* body language is saying to other people. We sometimes think that when we are feeling sad or annoyed or anxious, that is perfectly obvious to our friends and lovers, when in fact they are clueless. Sometimes—especially with romantic partners—they don't know how we feel because *they don't want to know*. But it is not just their fault. Often our own body language just isn't that obvious. The signs are not there, even for the people genuinely interested in seeing them.

14.

Unconscious, Gut-Level Lie Detection?

At some gut level, do you really know when someone is lying?

I'm the skunk at the garden party when it comes to statements about humans' ability to detect deception. There are people like Paul Ekman who claims he can detect high-stakes lies at very high levels of accuracy and can train others to do the same. There are many book authors who also pretend that they can teach you to tell when someone is lying, sometimes with ludicrous tips (e.g., is the person you suspect touching his or her nose?). They probably make much more money than I do from writing books on deception.

My belief is that people are barely better than chance at knowing when people are lying and when they are telling the truth. That is based on a review paper Charlie Bond and I published based on a statistical analysis (meta-analysis) of every study ever done -- there were hundreds of them -- on human deception detection success. We found that if you ask people directly whether someone is lying or telling the truth, they will, on the average, only be correct about 54% of the time, when they could get 50% correct just by guessing.

But in the *New York Times*, in "The search for our inner lie detectors," a reporter raised the question of whether we might know more at an unconscious level than is apparent from our explicit judgments of whether or not a person is lying. Since he quoted me in the article, I thought I'd tell you a bit more about my previous research on this topic. You can find a more complete discussion of my own research on this topic (and other people's) in <u>*The Hows and Whys of Lies*</u>; here I'll just share some highlights.

In most of my studies of deception-detection, my colleagues and I showed people video clips of people who were either lying or telling the truth. (I'll call the people viewing the video clips *judges* of deception, in the layperson sense of the term. In some studies, the judges interacted face-to-face with the people who were lying or telling the truth, rather than just watching them on video, and sometimes they listened to audio clips or read transcripts.) We always ask the judges to tell us whether they think the person in the clip was lying or telling the truth. That's a direct, explicit measure of deception-detection.

We also ask the judges other questions – *indirect* questions. Here are some examples of questions we asked them about their impressions of the persons who were lying or telling the truth:

- How ambivalent did the person seem?
- How comfortable did the person seem?

We also asked the judges about their own feelings after each clip that they watched (or heard or read, or each interaction they had). For example, we asked them:

- How comfortable did you feel?
- How suspicious did you feel?
- How confident do you feel about your judgment?
- Did you feel that you got enough information?

We did studies like these with adults and we also did a developmental deception-detection study with people ranging in age from 6th graders through college students. In almost every instance, we found that *people could distinguish lies from truths more effectively by their answers to all their indirect questions than they could by*

71

telling us directly whether they thought someone was lying or telling the truth.

For example, people are more likely to feel comfortable and confident in their judgments, and more likely to feel that they got enough information, and less likely to feel suspicious, when the person they were judging was telling the truth than when that person was lying. They also think the person they are judging seemed less comfortable and more ambivalent when that person was lying than when that person was telling the truth. All those distinctions are sharper than the distinctions made by direct judgments of whether the person was deceptive, or just how deceptive the person seemed.

In sum, when people are asked directly whether someone is lying or telling the truth, their accuracy is just a little bit better than chance. But when you ask them a less direct question, that does not involve calling someone a liar, then they are a little better than they were before. They still aren't great at separating the liars from the truth-tellers, but they are better than they were with the most explicit questions.

My favorite study on this topic was not my own, but a doctoral dissertation of a student in my lab, Eric Anderson. His study was based on that awkward couple thing, where one person in the couple points to someone else and asks the partner – Do you think that person is attractive?

Anderson brought people into the lab and showed them pictures of other people. For each picture, he asked them whether they thought the person was attractive. Behind a one-way mirror, their romantic partner was watching them. So was a total stranger, of the same sex as their romantic partner. (So if a woman was watching her boyfriend, then the other person watching her boyfriend was also a woman.) But, importantly, the people watching from behind the mirror could not see the pictures of the people being evaluated for their attractiveness. They were simply asked whether the person answering the questions ("Do you think that person is attractive?") was lying or telling the truth. They were also asked some of the other indirect questions listed above.

When asked directly whether the person was lying or telling the truth, the romantic partners were barely better than chance, at 52%. The complete strangers weren't all that great at deception-detection either, but at 58%, they were better than the romantic partners. So who knows better whether your partner thinks someone else is attractive – you or a stranger? If we go by direct questions about lying or telling the truth, the answer is that perfect strangers know better.

But what about those indirect measures? Both the romantic partners and the strangers felt like they got more of the information that they needed, and they also felt more comfortable, when the person they were judging was telling the truth than when they were lying. They felt more suspicious when the person was lying than when the person was telling the truth. That means that they all achieved a certain level of indirect deception detection. Again, their indirect deception detection was not that great but it was better than their direct deception detection (based on their answers to the explicit question of whether the person was lying).

Now here's the final twist: Even though the romantic partners were *worse* than the strangers at detecting deception when asked directly whether the person was lying, they were better than the strangers at indirect deception detection. Their feelings of comfort and of having gotten enough information, and their judgments of suspiciousness, separated the lies from the truths more effectively than the strangers' judgments did.

Here's my final paragraph about this research, from _The Hows and Whys of Lies_:

What we do not yet understand, but would very much like to explore, is this disconnect between partners' direct ratings of deceptiveness and their gut intuitions. Are the partners not aware that their feelings of confidence and suspiciousness and perceptions of other people's suspiciousness are varying in ways that could be meaningful? Do they have any clue at all that there could be a link between these kinds of feelings and whether or not their partner is lying? And if they were clued in on this clue, would it even matter? Could they use that information effectively, or would their attempts to use it undermine the process whereby they form these meaningful impressions and intuitions? And finally, the more sinister question: If they could use this information to find out who their partners really did find attractive, would they really want to know this? Maybe they should just let sleeping frauds lie.

15.

Can't Keep Your Story Straight: Maybe Not Such a Great Cue to Deception After All

What we think we know about lying isn't always so.

In Ferguson, Missouri, Darren Wilson, the white police officer who shot and killed the unarmed Black man, Michael Brown, walked away from any charges. The grand jury made its decisions, and no files were charged. As I listened to the prosecutor's lengthy statement, my ears perked up when he mentioned the importance of the consistency of the witnesses' statements. Some, he said, were consistent over time, and others were not. The clear implication was that the inconsistent statements were lies.

I remembered that two Swedish researchers, Pars Anders Granhag and Leif Stromwall, have conducted research on the topic of the relative consistency of statements over time, depending on whether the statements were made by witnesses who were lying or telling the truth. In their research, participants watched a staged event involving a robbery and a stabbing. The witnesses, who lied or told the truth about that they had watched, had time to plan their statements. Over a period of 11 days, they were each questioned three different times about what they had witnessed.

Here's what the authors have to say about what they found:

1. People who viewed all three interviews were no more accurate at knowing which witnesses were lying and which were telling the truth than those who watched only the first interview.

2. Of all the people who watched the three statements, 60% said that they used the consistency of the statements to decide whether the witnesses were truthful. (If they thought the three statements were consistent, they thought the witness was truthful.)
3. Of those 60% who used consistency as their criterion for truthfulness, "half perceived the three statements to be consistent over time, whereas the other half perceived the *same* three statements to be inconsistent over time."
4. Most importantly, the authors noted: "when comparing *truthful and deceptive consecutive statements* we found them to be *equally consistent*." [my emphasis]

Why might liars give statements that are just as consistent over time as those of truthtellers? There are several possibilities. One suggested by the authors is that "liars will try to *repeat* what they have said in previous interrogations..., while truth-tellers will try to *reconstruct* what they at some point in time actually experienced."

There are important ways in which the controlled research studies were not analogous to what happened in Ferguson. So we need to be cautious in the implications we draw from the findings. What we can say, though, is people's intuitive ideas about how liars behave are not always supported by systematic research. That's so not just for laypersons, but also for professionals such as judges and police officers.

References:

Granhag, P. A., & Stromwall, L. A. (1999). Repeated interrogations – stretching the deception detection paradigm. *Expert Evidence, 7*, 163-174.

Granhag, P. A., & Stromwall, L. A. (1999). Repeated interrogations: Verbal and non-verbal cues to deception. *Applied Cognitive Psychology, 16*, 243-257.

16.

If You Watch 'Lie to Me,' Will You Become More Successful at Detecting Lies?

Truth or hype in the science of lie-detection?

I know, the TV show *Lie to Me* is toast, but with streaming and such, we can all have our toast and eat it, too. But will it make us big and strong lie detectors?

When FOX first promoted the show in 2009, it claimed that it was "inspired by the scientific discoveries of Dr. Paul Ekman, a real-life specialist who can read clues embedded in the human face, body, and voice to expose both the truth and lies in criminal investigations." So would viewers who watched the show learn to become more accurate at distinguishing lies from truths?

That's what deception researcher Tim Levine and his colleagues set out to determine when the show had just begun to air. They randomly assigned college students to watch either the series premier of *Lie to Me* or of *Numb3rs* (another crime drama in which Stanford math whizzes are the hero crime-solvers). In a third condition (the control), students did not watch any particular TV show as part of the study.

All the participants then watched 12 videotapes of people who were tempted to cheat at a trivia game and thereby get a cash prize. Some did - and then lied about it in a subsequent interview. The others did not cheat and told the truth during the interview. On the 12 tapes, half of the people were lying and the others were telling the truth. Participants watched each clip, then recorded their judgment of whether or not the person was lying. By chance, participants would be right 50% of the time. Here are their actual accuracy scores:

60% *Lie to Me*

62% *Numb3rs*

65% Control

The differences were not statistically significant, so we can't conclude that people who watched *Lie to Me* actually did worse at labeling lies as lies and truths as truths, but they surely did no better than anyone else.

Many studies of human lie detection show that people have a "truth bias" - they see other people as truthful more often than they should. (Arguably, this particular bias is not necessarily a bad thing - maybe it is better to err on the side of believing people than disbelieving them.) In studies such as Levine's, truth bias is measured simply by computing the percentage of clips that participants judged to be truths. In fact, half of the clips were truths, so an unbiased score would be 50%. Here are the actual 'truth bias' scores for the three conditions:

51% *Lie to Me*

58% *Numb3rs*

59% Control

The difference between the viewers of *Lie to Me* and the participants in the other condition was a real one - the *Lie to Me* viewers were less inclined to judge the people on the videotapes as truthful. Those truth bias scores sum across judgments of both truths and lies. The bigger difference, though, was for the truths - *Lie to Me* viewers were much less likely than the other participants to see the actual truths as truthful.

So why didn't viewers of a show supposedly based on a real scientist and actual scientific research do better at detecting deception? Maybe they needed to watch more than one episode - but the differences were in the direction of worse accuracy for the *Lie to Me* viewers.

It is not surprising that promotions for TV shows engage in hype. Levine and his colleagues suggest that it is not just the show that has been oversold but the science of lie-detection as well. That's what Charlie Bond and I concluded, too, on the basis of our series of papers on lie-detection accuracy. In our review of hundreds of studies of skill at detecting deception, we found an average accuracy rate of only 54% (when a chance level would have been 50%). One of the papers in that collection is a study in which my colleagues and I compared the lie-detection judgments of experienced law enforcement officers to those of college students. The law enforcement officers were no more accurate - they only thought they were. (They were more confident.)

Reference:

Levine, T. R., Serota, K. B., & Shulman, H. C. (2010). The impact of Lie to Me on viewers' actual ability to detect deception. *Communication Research, 37*, 847-856.

17.

Suppose You Could Know Exactly What Other People Were Thinking and Feeling: Would You Want to?

Be careful what you wish for.

Technology seems to be advancing at a record pace. Claims about possibilities that once seemed unthinkable are now commonplace. Maybe, it has been suggested, technology can distinguish gay people from straight people from facial features. Maybe technology can detect emotions from the face, or clues that a person is lying. And maybe that technology can be incorporated into something wearable, such as glasses. Then we could wear those glasses and learn things about other people that, just a short time ago, we could never have fathomed.

Suppose all this were true, and you could know, with 100% accuracy, what another person was thinking and feeling. Does that sound appealing to you?

First, think about this from the perspective of the person whose once-private thoughts and feelings are now knowable to everyone with access to the technology. Anyone could now know, with total certainty, when you are lying and when you are telling the truth.

To me, it sounds appalling.

It is bad enough that my nonverbal behaviors can give away emotions I'd rather keep to myself, even to people with no technological assistance at reading them. Under this Brave

New World scenario, I would have no control whatsoever over what people knew.

Sometimes, I'd like to think, I have good reasons for keeping things to myself. In some instances, I'm still dealing with issues myself, and not yet ready to share my feelings with others. Other times, I don't want other people to know what I'm thinking or feeling about them because it is not very kind, and I'd rather not hurt them with those painful truths.

Now consider the question from the perspective of the person who gets to wear the magical glasses and know exactly what other people are thinking and feeling. Does that sound good? I used to do a lot of research on deception, and I learned that in many of the lies of everyday life, people pretend to feel more positively than they really do. If they dislike you, they may try to cover that up. If they are bored by what you are saying, they might make the effort to appear interested. Do you really want to know how people really do feel about you?

I don't do much work on deception these days, but I've been thinking about this because a reporter asked me what I thought about the implications of having technological devices that could detect deception with perfect accuracy.

His question reminded me of my very first job interview as a new PhD. I gave a talk at the University of Pennsylvania, and the eminent sociologist Erving Goffman showed up to listen. I was talking about the detection of deception. When my talk was over, I was greatly relieved to be done with it, and was headed to the bathroom for a different kind of relief. Goffman followed me down the hallway until I was at the door of the ladies' room. He was still a few paces behind me and called out, "What do you think would happen if we learned to detect lies perfectly?"

I thought to myself, "we'll never get that good," but I paused because I wasn't sure I wanted to say that. While I thought for a moment, he said, "You know what I think? I think we'll *never* get that good!"

I still think that's true, and it is true of the technological detection of deception as well as the kind of deception detection I was discussing in my talk – unaided human lie detection.

A big problem is that sometimes the technology is going to get it wrong. The gravity of the consequences depend on how the technology is being used. Is it in a criminal context, in which a person's guilt or innocence is being judged? Will technological lie-detection tools become so inexpensive and portable/wearable that they become ubiquitous and people use them in everyday interactions? Even in casual settings, getting led astray by inaccurate technology can be consequential, especially if the technology gets it wrong in a smearing way – declaring someone deceptive who is actually telling the truth.

If technology gets used in those kinds of ways, it will probably be experienced as an invasion of privacy. It is also one more barrier to direct, unmediated, human-to-human interaction. It is one more way in which we are not fully present with one another as fellow humans.

Another issue is that not only will technology get things wrong some of the time, but we humans won't know when it is getting things right and when it is getting things wrong. People are rightly offended, sometimes even incensed, when they are falsely accused of lying in everyday life. Imagine how much angrier they will feel when some piece of technology damned them, and some other human believed the technology over them.

I also wonder whether our ability to detect deception without the aid of any technology – which is already fairly <u>unimpressive</u> – could become even worse if we start depending on technology. Maybe we would become even less attentive to other people's behavior and their feedback if we decided to lean on technological answers.

The movie *Liar, Liar*, starring Jim Carrey, was based on the promising premise of a lawyer who could not tell a lie for 24 hours. I thought the follow-through was disappointing. With that premise, it could have been a whole lot funnier. But that's where total transparency belongs – in the movies.

V.

Lying and Detecting Lies in Relationships

18.

Do Relationships Need Lies to Survive?

Save a relationship with a lie? Not a serious lie.

Recently, a reporter from the *Daily Mail* discovered my new book, Behind the Door of Deceit: Understanding the Biggest Liars in Our Lives, and got in touch about an interview. She had a hunch, she said, that romantic relationships need a dash of deceit to survive.

First, let me answer the reporter's question with an anecdote. Because I studied deception for so long, and have found in my work that lying (or, at least the telling of little lies) is ordinary rather than extraordinary, occasionally I get challenged. A conversation partner or student or someone in an audience at one of my talks will claim that they never lie. Even more interestingly, some will vow to spend the next several weeks without telling any lies at all. I never suggest or encourage this, but I do ask them to tell me about their experiences.

Only a few people have actually followed through with their personal experiments in honesty, but the result has been the same each time. They have to call it off after a few days and go back and apologize. They say they are sorry to the person whose party invitation they declined with the honest response that the person's parties are always boring - or that the host him or herself is boring. They ask for forgiveness for saying to the friend who asked that she really does look like she gained weight. They try to make it up to the coworker whose contributions they described, in all honesty, as not up to par.

I draw a big line between little lies and big ones. <u>Serious lies</u> - the big-time betrayals of trust - are probably never good for relationships of any kind. Little lies are often a different matter entirely. Sometimes people tell these lies not because they don't value honesty, but because telling the truth conflicts with something else they value, such as being compassionate or loyal or reassuring.

As I've noted before, <u>romantic relationships are hotbeds for serious lies</u>. Serious lies are often told by and to other close relationship partners, too, such as parents. For example, when parents hide a grim diagnosis of a grandparent's illness from an adolescent, sometimes that grandchild will still feel badly about the deception many years later. There is an intriguing exception, though, to the rule that the most serious lies are told by and to the people who are closest to us: In the 238 stories of serious lies that we collected, only 6 of them involved a best friend.

The reporter wrote an interesting story on the questions she asked me; you can read it <u>here</u>. Because she sent me her questions in advance, I wrote out some answers, so I thought I'd share them with you. (DM means Daily Mail.)

DM: How prevalent is lying in romantic relationships?

Bella: It depends on whether we are talking about the little lies of everyday life or the big, serious lies. We have a good idea for the little lies. In romantic relationships that are not married relationships, people <u>lie in one out of every three conversations</u>. With a spouse, they lie in one out of every 10 conversations. We don't know whether people become more honest as they become more serious about the relationship, or whether they are more honest from the outset with the person they will eventually marry.

It is different for <u>serious lies</u>. When people lie about something big - such as an affair, or about some other terrible thing they did, or just about anything else they consider serious - they are more likely to tell those lies to the people they care about the most. Our spouses and the other people we feel closest to are the ones who have the highest expectations for us. That means it is especially hard to tell them that you have fallen so short of those expectations.

DM: Are all lies bad?
Bella: It might seem so in the abstract. But we live in the real world. We might value honesty and want to be honest, but we sometimes value other qualities at the same time, such as compassion or loyalty. Sometimes, <u>two noble goals come into conflict</u>. If you tell the truth, you will be unkind, and if you say something kind, it will be a lie. Sometimes when people lie to the ones they love, it is because they are valuing something else more than honesty. Maybe they are trying to be loyal, or to avoid hurting the other person's feelings. Maybe they think that the other person isn't in a good enough place, emotionally, to hear a painful truth.

Liars sometimes claim to tell lies so as to spare the other person from pain. Sometimes they really mean it. But they can also be using that as an excuse to give themselves an out.

DM: Why do people lie to their partners and what do they lie about?
Bella: Sometimes people tell what I call "<u>kind-hearted lies</u>." Those are the lies told to spare someone else's feelings or make them look better to others or feel better. Examples include: "I know just how you feel;" "you did the right thing;" "you look great." If you care about someone, you are more likely to tell them those kinds of lies.

Many of the other little lies of everyday life are told to make the liars look better or feel better or get what they want. Those are the self-serving lies. They can be told because the liars really are acting in a self-centered way, but there's another reason, too. Sometimes liars claim to be smarter or kinder or more accomplished than they really are because they are trying to impress the other person. So, they puff up their own image because they care so much about what the other person thinks of them. They want to create a good impression, but they are not sure whether their true self will be good enough. So they lie. Probably more of this kind of lying goes on when potential partners are first getting to know each other.

Serious lies are a whole other matter. When we asked people about the most serious lie they ever told to anyone, and the most serious lie anyone ever told to them, they described lies about many different things. But the most common were lies about affairs.

19.

Infidelity: Who Are the Real Cheaters?

Decades of research reveal surprising truths about infidelity.

Recently I wrote about a study showing that people in a serious romantic relationship, as compared to single (uncoupled) people, have two fewer people they believe they can call on in times of severe crisis. One of the best opinion pieces I read about the study was by Laurie Essig, who addressed the question of why this even matters. One answer was that romantic partners are not always faithful. Those who are betrayed and end up feeling hurt and abandoned would do well to have other people in their lives they did not neglect in order to focus on *The One*.

But just how often do romantic partners actually stray? We can never really know, of course. Even in representative national surveys, we can only go by are people's own admissions of their infidelity. Happily, though, in a recent issue of the journal ***Contexts***, Deborah Carr reported the results of one national survey that has been ongoing for decades.

From 1973 through 2008, a representative sample of Americans has been asked to give their opinions about infidelity. (They are not the same people each year.) For example, they respond to the question, "A married person having sexual relations with someone other than their spouse is..." with the answer choices being, "always wrong," "almost always wrong," "sometimes wrong," or "not wrong at all." From 1991 through 2008, survey participants who had ever been married were also asked to indicate whether they had ever cheated on their spouse. See how accurately you can guess their responses by answering these 5 questions. The answers follow.

1. True or False:

Over time, Americans have become less judgmental about cheating. Specifically, from 1973 through 2008, the percent who say that "a married person having sexual relations with someone other than their spouse is *always* wrong" has steadily *decreased*.

2. True or False:

The number of ever-married men who admit to having cheated on their spouse is *nearly 50%*.

3. True or False:

Among those who have ever been married, *more men than women* admit to having cheated on their spouse.

4. True or False:

Men and women are becoming *more similar* in their rates of cheating (or at least in their self-reports of their rates of cheating).

5. True or False:

Fewer than half of all cheaters believe that marital infidelity is always wrong.

Answers:

1. False. The percent of Americans who say that cheating is always wrong has actually *increased*, from around 65% in 1973 to about 81% in 2008. (Data are from the first graph in the article.)

2. False. Between 1991 and 2008, somewhere between about *20% to 25%* of *men* admit to having cheated on their wives.

3. True. Rates of admitted infidelity for *women* have ranged between about *10% and 15%*, compared to the 20 to 25% for men.

4.True. Among people 65 and older, women were only half as likely as men to say that they cheated. Among people ages 18 to 24, women were *81% as likely as men* to admit to infidelity.

5. False. Among people who have admitted to cheating, *64% say that infidelity is always wrong*. Of those who claim to have always been faithful, though, the corresponding number is 86%.

20.

Spotting a Cheater: How Long Do You Have to Know a Person Before You Can Do It Accurately?

Busted at first sight?

Most people who are cheating on their romantic partners don't want to be caught. They don't want their partners to recognize their infidelity, and they don't want other people to be able to tell, either.

So is it possible for people to just watch a couple and know whether one of the partners is cheating on the other? If so, how long would you have to know the possible cheater? Would you need to be a close friend or maybe a relative who has known the person their whole life? Would you need to be the person who is getting cheated on?

The romantic partner who is getting betrayed by their partner may well be the last to know. Often, they just really do not want to know – they are motivated to believe that their partner would never do that to them. Careful research shows that romantic partners are sometimes worse than complete strangers at knowing when their partner is lying.

In a recent set of studies, psychologists made the brazen prediction that total strangers could recognize, at a level that is better than chance, whether someone is cheating on their romantic partner, and that they could figure that out by watching the couple interact for only about four minutes!

In each of the two studies, college student couples interacted with each other for about 3-5 minutes. Their interactions were videotaped. One person in each couple completed a measure assessing any physical or emotional infidelity to their partner. (Of course, their answers were for the researchers' eyes only.) The videotapes of the interactions were shown to complete strangers, who were asked to focus on the key person (the one who reported on his or her own infidelity). Those strangers reported their impressions of whether that person was cheating on their partner, by answering questions such as "How likely do you think this person has had sexual intercourse with someone other than his/her partner?" In the second study, the strangers also indicated their impressions of how committed to their romantic partner the person seems to be, and how trustworthy the person seems.

Based on only about 4 minutes of observing the couples, the strangers could tell, to a moderately successful degree, who was cheating and who was not. Their impressions correlated significantly with the key persons' own reports of their cheating. The strangers seemed to use their sense of the person's trustworthiness and commitment to their partner as clues to whether they were cheating.

The couples in the study and the strangers who observed them were all college students, and the strangers were almost all women, so as social scientists like to say, "More research is needed." It is interesting, though, that people can get a pretty good sense of who is a committed romantic partner and who is a cheater from such a "thin slice" of their behavior.

Reference:

Lambert, N. M., Mulder, S., & Fincham, F. (2014). Thin slices of infidelity: Determining whether observers can pick out cheaters from a video clip of their interaction and what tips them off. *Personal Relationships, 21,* 612-619.

21.

Manti Te'o and the Revenge of the Romantic Fantasy

A sap for sappy love stories

Now that Manti Te'o's fake dead girlfriend has been exposed as just plain fake, pundits and reporters and bloggers and tweeters are savoring the opportunity to pile on the ridicule. The romantic fantasy has been exposed as a hoax, and a consensus seems to be emerging on how to characterize the whole charade – it is a really bad *Lifetime* movie.

True enough. But why all the wallowing in the sappiness and why all the credulous swallowing of the incredible storylines *before* the scam got debunked?

It is usually such a sure thing, this matrimania writ-large. The love stories right out of *Love Story*. When I wrote *Singled Out* in 2006 and bemoaned all of the venues that invite the over-the-top celebrations of weddings and coupling and marriage, I quipped that there was at least one night a week, in one domain, when Americans could count on getting a break from it all: "They could turn on *Monday Night Football* in full confidence that the game will not end with a wedding."

Since 2006, matrimania has jumped the shark. Now there seems to be no venue, in the media or in our everyday lives, which is safe from sappy love stories.

In case you haven't already read about the Te'o story elsewhere, here are just a few of the badly-written lines (from here and here):

- When Te'o and fake-girlfriend Lennay Kekua first met, "Their stares got pleasantly tangled, then Manti Te'o extended his hand to the stranger with a warm smile and soulful eyes."
- Lennay had a "volleyball-type of physique...She was athletic, tall, beautiful. Long hair."
- When fake-girlfriend was in a coma, her relatives told Te'o that "at her lowest points, as she fought to emerge from a coma, her breathing rate would increase at the sound of his voice."
- Lennay's last words to Manti were, "I love you."

Now, finally, the matrimania is biting back. Was Te'o a victim, a perpetrator, or a bit of both? Regardless of the answer, he was a sap. He bought into the romantic fantasies that elevate one type of relationship above all others. The ones that reliably elicit an outsized reaction to hackneyed tale. Maybe he, or some perpetrators who saw themselves as his boosters and friends, thought that such a story would make him an even more seductive candidate for a Heisman Trophy. Maybe they just craved the rush of other people's emotions – their awe at what a wonderful guy Te'o seemed to be (never mind that he never was there for Lennay in person, after the car crash or during the cancer or at her funeral), their sharing of his despair over the tragic loss of "the most beautiful girl" he had ever met (even though he never did meet the woman who never did exist).

The Notre Dame coach was also duped, big time. After the dramatic football game that Te'o played in rather than going to his soul-mate's funeral, "head coach Brian Kelly awards the game ball to Lennay Kekua, handing it to Te'o to 'take back to Hawaii.'"

Even more devastating, legions of reporters were saps, too. All those treacly romantic twists and turns? They ate them all up.

Now will romance and marriage and coupling get put in their place? Will the greatest awards go to the greatest talents and achievements and not the people claiming the most matrimaniacal tales? I doubt it. Not yet. A few more stories like this one, though, and who knows.

22.

When You Are the Last to Know You've Been Duped

Sometimes what hurts is not just the lie or the cover-up, but realizing that other people knew you were being deceived before you did.

For years, I collected people's stories of the most serious lie they ever told anyone and the most serious lie that had ever been told to them. (See more <u>here</u>.) When I read the stories of the people who had been duped, I expected to hear expressions of great pain over having been deceived, and over whatever the lie had been about—affairs, money, livelihood, illnesses, kinship, love, and even life and death.

There was another theme, though, that was less predictable but oh, so powerful: Sometimes when a person first figures out they have been duped, they learn something *else* at the same time—that not only did they not know about what was going on, but that all sorts of people *did* know, long before they did. The "in-crowd"—the people who knew before the dupe did—included people who, by the usual psychology of disclosure rules, should not have known.

Two examples (from <u>*Behind the Door of Deceit: Understanding the Biggest Liars in Our Lives*</u>) illustrate the power of disclosure rules and what happens when they are broken. The first is about an affair:

One young woman described her boyfriend Bill's affair with another woman. The dupe's best friends were Mary (Bill's cousin) and Lynn. The person who was betrayed told us that soon after discovering the infidelity, "I was talking to Lynn and I go, 'Wait, do you know about this?' For some reason, it just occurred to me that Bill could have told Mary and Mary could have told Lynn. And they were supposed to be my two best friends and so they knew the whole time and they never told me..."

The dupe's implicit knowledge of the rules of disclosure led her to her accurate suspicions. Of course Bill would tell Mary, because they were cousins. And then of course Mary would tell Lynn because they were friends. And then Mary and Lynn would tell the dupe because they were *her* two best friends. But wait: They never told her! And they knew the entire time. The consequences for the friendship alliances were profound. Mary and Lynn shared a secret and kept it from their friend; ultimately, *they* became best friends and the dupe was pushed completely out of the picture.

The second is from a high-school student who was the last to find out a profoundly important piece of family news:

It was about last May and my mom had cancer. And during the time I had an important tennis game and I had been taking SATs, too, so everybody in my family knew that she had cancer for three weeks before they told me....And I never really told anybody but I felt really bad that I wasn't told....They didn't want anything bothering me. But it really did, so I felt like, everybody else in my family knew—all my siblings, including even my younger sister.

Disclosure rules have their own emotional logic. We understand them intuitively. Younger sisters, for example, should not learn about family matters of life and death before their older brothers.

Examples like the ones I just recounted, in which someone who should have been one of the first to know is instead one of the last, are the most dramatic illustrations of the power of disclosure rules. They are instances in which the breach of the rules destroys intimacy. But the flip side is significant, too—when someone is unexpectedly bumped *up* in the pecking order. They are let in on something before someone else who should have known sooner. When that happens, the breach of the rules of disclosure results in a *deepening* of intimacy.

Here's an example:

A friend of mine told me about a conversation she had with a colleague. He had just been offered a job. It was a big deal to get the offer and it would be a big deal to accept it. Would he take the offer seriously? Would he move across the country for that job? Then she casually asked, "So what does your wife think?" You know where this is going: He hadn't told her. When this very significant event happened in his life, he told his colleague and friend at work, and mulled it over with her, before he ever told his wife.

I think that disclosure rules represent one of the most underappreciated signs of intimacy—and their breach an underappreciated sign of potential doom. In academic journals, there are tons of studies on self-disclosure and some on secrecy, but this is something else: Disclosure rules are not just about whether you share secrets or personal feelings with someone else—they are about the *order* in which you are, or are not, let into the inner circle. I don't know of any scholarly research on that.

I rarely read articles or blog posts touting "Top 10 Signs of Intimacy," or "Top Signs Your Relationship Is in Trouble," but I'll bet that those of you who have skimmed such pieces have found the same thing: The power of disclosure rules is not recognized.

23.

Friends and Lovers: Is There a "Knew It All Along" Effect?

Sometimes you don't acknowledge what you know, even to yourself.

Back when I was studying the psychology of deceiving and getting deceived, my colleagues and I did some research in which we asked people to tell us, in detail, about the most serious lie they ever told to anyone and the most serious lie anyone ever told them. (You can read some of their stories here.) It will not surprise you that more serious lies were about affairs than anything else. There was a certain theme I found intriguing in the stories of the people whose partners were cheating on them - they suggested that once they became certain that their partner was cheating, all sorts of things seemed to fall into place. It was as if they "knew it all along," but had not let themselves acknowledge what was going on until they had to.

There was no way to know from that study alone what was actually happening. Did they just tell themselves that they knew it all along so they would not feel like complete and total dupes? Or at some level, did they really know?

People in close romantic relationships often believe that they know better than anyone else when their partner is lying. Sometimes they can even describe to you what they believe to be the tell-tale clues. But thinking that you can tell doesn't mean that you can tell. (In fact, in a review my colleagues and I did of all the available studies of accuracy and confidence, we found that people who were confident about their judgments of deceptiveness were no more or less likely to be correct in their judgments than people who were not confident.)

The intuitive case for believing that you know when your partner is lying better than anyone else does is that you spend so much time with that person and observe that person so carefully (at least in theory). Perhaps that greater exposure and experience could help if it were the only thing figuring into your insights into your partner's deceptiveness. But of course, it is not. One of the most important additional factors is motivation. What would it mean to see through to the truth instead of the fantasy that your partner is selling to you? If you are worried that you might not like what you see, you may not be so great at all at recognizing what is right there in front of you.

In fact, a graduate student of mine a while back, Eric Anderson, did a clever dissertation (described here) in which he had people answer the dreaded question, "Do you think that person over there is attractive?" The romantic partners did *worse* at knowing whether the answers were truthful or deceptive than total strangers did. At some level, though, they did seem to know the truth. When they were asked indirect questions (for example, "did you get enough information from the person's answer?"), the partners were actually better than the strangers at distinguishing the lies from the truths. That is, they realized that they had not gotten enough information when their partner was lying (even though they didn't know for sure that their partner was lying) and they felt that they *did* get enough information when their partner was telling the truth.

Probably because of my interest in single life, I've always been more interested in what friends know and don't know than what romantic partners do. As friends get to know each other better, do they become more insightful about each other's honesty and dishonesty? My colleagues (Eric Anderson and Matthew Ansfield) and I assessed the deception-detection abilities of 52 pairs of friends when they had known each other for just one month, and then again about five months later. (The study is here.) When we just compared the deception detection accuracy of all 52 pairs the second time around to their accuracy when they only knew each other for a month, it looked like nothing happened. They got no better or worse over time.

As friendships progress, some of them deepen and others - well, they don't. We thought that might matter. So we looked separately at the pairs of friends who had become closer after five months, and those who had become less close. Now things started to happen. The friends who were becoming closer were also becoming better at separating each other's lies from their truths. Not so for the friends who were growing apart. They just became more distrusting overall. They became more inclined to believe that their friend was lying, even when that person was telling the truth.

The theme of today's "hot topic" is "friendships are complicated, too," so now let me introduce an intriguing complication. Does a friend's insightfulness depend on what it is that the other person is trying to hide?

It does indeed. In another study (also here), Weylin Sternglanz and I videotaped people as they honestly described experiences that had made them feel happy or sad or angry. They also described other experiences that made them feel happy or sad or angry, but they tried to conceal their true feelings rather than express them clearly. Close friends, less close friends, and strangers watched the tapes and tried to figure out how the people on the tapes really did feel.

When no one was trying to hide anything, the friends were always better than the strangers at knowing how the people on the tape really did feel. The closer friends were better than the strangers, and the less close friends were better, too.

If you want to test your psychological intuition, take a guess about the relative accuracy of the close friends, the less close friends, and the strangers when the people on the tape were trying to conceal negative feelings (sadness or anger). When you've told yourself your answer, then continue reading.

The people who did the *worst* at discerning how the people on the tape were feeling when they were trying to hide their sadness or their anger were the *close friends*. The close friends were even a shade worse at the task than the complete strangers. The people who did really well were the less close friends.

It will take additional research to nail down a definitive explanation for these results, so I'll just mention a few of the possibilities that Sternglanz and I considered. What if the feelings of sadness or anger had something to do with the friend? It might be more threatening to a closer friend than to a less close friend to realize that a friend is mad at you or disappointed with you. So if you are that closer friend, maybe you just don't see that negativity.

Or maybe closer friends are more inclined to allow one another a zone of privacy - maybe they can tell when the other person doesn't want to talk about something, and they leave it alone. Or maybe closer friends, if they recognized the anger or sadness, would feel more responsible for doing something about it than less close friends. If they don't want to do what it would take to deal with their friend's distress, then maybe the easy answer is not to recognize the distress. (That doesn't fit the ideal of the close friend, and it is not my preferred interpretation, but it is a possibility.)

The bottom line is that it *is* complicated with friends, as it is with lovers. Your special closeness and added experiences offer the *potential* to make you more insightful. That's just a potential, though. If you might not like what you see, maybe you just won't see it. There may come a time when denial is no longer an option. It is then that you may realize that, at some level, you knew it all along.

24.

What Friends Know that Others Don't

What friends see, and what they don't

In the very first course I ever taught as a faculty member, an undergraduate proposed a simple study. Dot Brauer wanted to show pairs of friends pictures of facial expressions and body postures to see how friends would compare to strangers in their reading of the nonverbal cues. Would two friends interpret the same nonverbal cues more similarly than two strangers?

You probably know intuitively what lots of research has shown - friends are often similar to each other in many ways. They often share attitudes, values, and interests. They are often the same sex and about the same age. Of course, there are lots of fascinating exceptions. The general rule, though, is not surprising.

But would it apply to the ways that friends interpret their interpersonal worlds? Even without consulting with each other, would two friends look at the same facial expression or body posture and think the same thing about what that person was feeling?

In the study that Dot Brauer and I did, the answer - with regard to facial expressions (but not postures) - was yes. Two friends were highly likely to agree with each other about the meaning of the facial expressions (they were given two choices each time), whereas pairs of strangers agreed no more often than would be expected by chance.

We wanted to know more about the pairs of friends, so we also asked each of them to indicate whether they discussed a variety of topics with each other. There were some very intimate topics on the list, as well as moderately intimate ones and some casual ones. That mattered. The more different topics the friends discussed with each other - especially the intimate ones - the more similar they were in how they interpreted facial expressions.

It was an intriguing study and we published it as a research note (not bad for Dot, who was an undergraduate and the first author!). In some ways, though, it was just suggestive. The friends were all women, we only recruited 20 friends (10 pairs), and the nonverbal communications were only in photographs, not videos.

Happily for me, more than a decade later, two colleagues who were then graduate students wanted to pursue this further. Matthew Ansfield and Kathy Bell and I videotaped women and men as they watched different kinds of slides. Some were pleasant (nice scenes, cute babies), some were unpleasant (scenes from surgery, images of burn victims), and others were unusual (odd photographic effects). Each person watched the slides alone and did not learn until later that they were being videotaped.

About a year later, 10 men and 12 women returned, and each brought a friend of the same sex. Everyone watched slides of people of their own sex. The slides always included the person in the study and strangers. So, the original participants watched videotapes of their own facial expressions and strangers' facial expressions. The companions watched the facial expressions of their friend (who appeared on the videotape) and the strangers.

Now we had six different measures of whether friends were similar to each other in how they interpreted facial expressions. Did they agree on what the person on the tape was feeling when that person was a stranger and was watching a pleasant slide? An unpleasant slide? An unsual slide? What about when that person was familiar because it was a friend or (for the original participants) the participant him- or herself?

For the friends who were women, the answer was clear and compelling. In all six instances, the female friends agreed with each other much more often than pairs of female strangers did. (For the statistical junkies out there, the intraclass correlations ranged from .50 to .80. Like I said, compelling!)

It was a whole different story for the pairs of men. In five of the six nonverbal interpretation tasks, the male friends agreed with each other no more often than pairs of men who were complete strangers to each other. The one exception occurred when the men were watching other men who were strangers to them and who were watching unpleasant slides.

Remember, all anyone ever sees in the videoclips are the participants' facial expressions. They have no idea which slides the participants are watching.

Just from watching 10 seconds of a person's facial expression, two female friends interpret that facial expression similarly. It doesn't matter whether they are watching someone familiar or unfamiliar, or whether the person in question is watching something pleasant or unpleasant or unusual. For the men, though, two friends only agree with each other more often than two strangers do if they are watching another man they do not know, who is looking at an unpleasant scene.

The smart and inquisitive students and colleagues just kept showing up, ready and eager to learn more about how friends compare to strangers in how they interpret each other's nonverbal behaviors and those of strangers. Weylin Sternglanz and I found that there are times when friends who are not so close are actually more insightful than the closer friends about what the other is feeling.

Later, my colleagues and I looked more specifically at deception. Are friends more honest with each other than they are with strangers? Over time, do friends learn to detect each other's deception more accurately? (Hint: Only some of them do.)

Something new is happening among scholars and in society more generally. After decades of obsessing about romantic relationships, more and more people are recognizing the importance of friendship in so many of our lives - including the lives of people who are single and coupled. For a very long time, hardly anyone asked me about the friendship theme in the research I had conducted over the past decades. Now, I get asked about that much more often.

Partly in response to that growing interest, I have put together five of my journal articles on friendship. The collection is a brief book called *Friendsight: What Friends Know that Others Don't*. Because these papers were originally published in academic journals, the results sections are blighted with statistics. However, the other sections (the introduction, the methods section, and the discussion section) should be readable to just about anyone.

25.

The Power and Peril of Hurt Feelings

Hurt feelings have an important place in the psychology of lying.

"You hurt my feelings." "I don't want to hurt your feelings." Those kinds of comments are commonplace. We know that hurt feelings are unpleasant, but somehow the matter of hurting someone's feelings seems like a small thing. We assume we can empathize or apologize or do whatever seems appropriate, then move on to more important matters.

I think we are wrong about that. Hurt feelings can be powerful and perilous.

I've thought a lot about hurt feelings both in the writing I do about single life and in my research on deceiving and detecting deceit. When I write about singlism (the stereotyping, stigmatizing, and discrimination against people who are single), readers get it when I point to the big ways in which single people are treated unfairly. Economic disadvantages, less access to affordable health insurance, discrimination in the housing market – all that is understandable.

When I describe ways in which single people get their feelings hurt, some readers scoff at the insignificance of it all. Why should single people care, they wonder, when they are excluded from social events by formerly single friends who are currently paired up? So what if other people think that single people don't have a life? What's the big deal when single people get assigned to the kids' table?

These everyday slights, though, can be painful. Over the past decade or so, social scientists have begun to study hurt feelings in earnest. They are examining the implications of hurt feelings for interpersonal conflict, aggression and violence, loyalty and infidelity, and health and well-being. They have found that hurt feelings are not just something we can brush off and forget about.

In my research on deception, I found that the desire to avoid hurting another person's feelings can be a powerful impediment to the truth. Imagine, for example, that there is a painting in front of you that you detest. A person walks into the room, points to the painting, and says: "That's one of my paintings. What do you think of it?"

My colleagues and I staged studies like this, and we found that people just could not bring themselves to tell the whole truth. They stonewalled, they said things that were purposefully misleading, and they soft-pedaled their true feelings. They did not tell the whole truth even in variations of the research in which we urged them to be honest, saying that the art students needed to learn what others really thought of their work. It was even worse when the art student was someone they liked – then their feedback was even further from the truth. (You can read about those studies and about what happens when the value of telling the truth clashes with the wish not to hurt another person's feelings in *When the truth hurts: Lying to be kind*.)

When people are trying to be polite and avoid hurting another person's feelings, it can be hard to tell how they really do feel. Sometimes that is exactly the point – the person who hates the painting doesn't want the artist to understand her true feelings. Researchers from France and the UK have extended research on our attempts to be polite into situations in which misunderstandings can be deadly. They have found that people can be overly polite about what they mean, and therefore confusing, even in such risky situations as advising patients on treatment options and flying planes in treacherous conditions. Our inclinations to avoid hurting feelings may be far more powerful and perilous than we realize.

Reference:

Bonnefon, J.-F., Feeney, A., & De Neys, W. (2011). The risk of polite misunderstandings. *Current Directions in Psychological Science, 20,* 321-324.

VI.

Lying and Detecting Lies in Special Contexts

26.

Do Audio-Only Press Briefings Make It Easier to Mislead?

Did it matter that the Trump White House tried banning video from some press briefings?

The decision of the White House to allow only audio recordings of some of the press briefings, instead of the full audiovisual airing, has caused a stir. People wanted to know why that was happening. Press Secretary Sean Spicer said that when the cameras are off, the discussions are more substantive. Jake Tapper of CNN said, "People in power like to hide things from the public."

In one of my articles on lying, Charlie Bond and I analyzed the results of every study ever conducted on adults' abilities to detect deception. We found more than 200 relevant articles. More than 24,000 people participated in the studies we reviewed; their role was to try to tell when other people were lying and when they were telling the truth.

All the study participants had to go by was what they were shown – typically, either an audiovisual recording of the liars and truth-tellers, an audio-only recording, or a recording of just the visuals (the liars' and truth-tellers' faces, and sometimes the rest of their bodies, too). They were trying to detect deception from nonverbal and verbal clues. They had no access to other ways of figuring out whether to trust the people they were judging – for example, by digging up relevant facts.

Usually, people in the studies observed a number of different statements. Half the time, the statements were true, and the rest of the time, they were lies. That means that if the participants were just guessing, they would be correct in their judgments 50% of the time.

If you have heard that people are not very good at detecting lies, that claim was probably based on the studies I just described. When Charlie Bond and I averaged the accuracy of the thousands of study participants across all the different ways the information was presented to them (such as audio-only, audiovisual, and visual only), we found that people were right 54% of the time. That's better than chance but hardly gives anyone bragging rights.

Now for the key results. Were people any less accurate at knowing when others were lying and when they were telling the truth when they had just an audio recording to go by rather than a full audiovisual recording?

The answer is no. When people only had access to an audio recording, they were right about their judgments of lies and truths 53% of the time. When they could hear and watch the people who were lying or telling the truth (full audiovisual), they were right 54% of the time. That difference was not statistically meaningful.

If Jake Tapper was correct in suggesting that the White House may have been trying to hide things by allowing only an audio recording and not a full audiovisual airing, the attempt was probably not successful. Or it wasn't if we can make the leap from the behavior of ordinary people who took part in the studies we reviewed to that of White House press briefers and those who judge their statements.

There's another way to look at people's judgments other than to ask whether they are accurate. It is also possible to see how often they think other people are telling the truth, regardless of whether those people are actually telling the truth or lying. Suppose that people who only get to hear an audio recording of the press briefings more often judge the press secretaries to be telling the truth than if they saw the full briefing, including the visuals. The White House might like that outcome.

Across all the judgments made by the thousands of people who participated in the studies we reviewed, there was a truth bias. If the participants were even-handed in their judgments of truthfulness, they would have judged half of the statements as truths and half as lies (which was the actual distribution of truths and lies). Instead, they guessed that about 56% of the statements were truths.

Were the people who only got to hear the audio recordings any more likely to believe what they were hearing than the people who got to see the full audiovisual recordings? Not significantly so. People who only heard the audio recordings thought that 59% of the statements they heard were truthful. Those who got to see and hear the full audiovisual recordings thought that 56% of the statements were truthful. Again, the difference was not statistically meaningful.

The White House has never made available only videotapes of the briefings, with no sound. But social scientists studying deception often include that condition, in part because some scholars have suggested that facial expressions and body movements can provide clues to deception. That's not what Charlie Bond and I found in our review. People who only got to watch videos, without any sound, were only correct 50% of the time. That's the same as if they were just guessing. The liars and truth-tellers who could only be seen and not heard were not perceived as very truthful, either. The study participants thought that 52% of the visual-only statements were truths. Remember that the participants who listened to audio-only recordings thought that 59% of the statements were truthful, and those who heard and watched the audiovisual recordings thought that 56% were truthful.

Occasionally, social scientists include a transcript condition, in which study participants make their judgments based only on a typed transcript of what the liars and truth-tellers said. There are no visual cues, and no tone of voice cues. Charlie Bond and I found only 5 studies comparing judgments based on transcripts to judgments based on full audiovisual recordings, and the findings were only about truth bias and not accuracy. The study participants who only had a typed transcript to go by were less likely to believe the statements than were the participants who got access to the full audiovisual recordings. Being disbelieved is probably not what anyone wants.

Reference:

Bond, Charles F., Jr., & DePaulo, Bella M. (2006). Accuracy of deception judgments. *Personality and Social Psychology Review, 10,* 214-234.

27.

Airport Screening Post-9/11: What Happens Before You Even Get to Any of the Machines

SPOT program: Screening of Passengers by Observational Techniques

Since 9/11, a lot has changed at airports. You already know about the scans of passengers and their luggage, the show-your-liquids and the take-off-your-shoes rules. But did you know that as you are standing in line at airport security, before you even get to any of the machines, you are already being monitored?

It doesn't happen everywhere. As of the last publicly available U.S. government report (GAO, May 2010), the program was ongoing in 161 airports in the U.S. It is an observational program called SPOT: Screening of Passengers by Observational Techniques. While you are standing in line waiting to be screened, two "behavior detection officers" are unobtrusively observing you. What they are trying to figure out, just by looking at you, is whether you may be up to no good.

This is an even more challenging task than the already formidable task of trying to tell whether someone is lying or telling the truth at that moment just from their nonverbal (and perhaps verbal) behavior. In the airport security instance, people are trying to tell whether you are behaving in a way that might indicate that you are *going to* do something bad, or maybe even catastrophic, such as blowing up the plane.

You can imagine the potential objections on grounds such privacy and accuracy (which I'll turn to next), but imagine, for a moment, that the technique were successful. It would mean that useful information could be obtained without adding any other machines or scans or disrobing or (for the vast majority of passengers) extending the time spent in the security process.

SPOT is actually not designed to replace any of the other layers of security. It is an added layer, one more chance to catch the bad guys before they do harm. At the core of SPOT is a checklist of behaviors that the behavior detection officers are trained to recognize. Each behavior is assigned a certain number of points. The officers memorize the list and the point-values, and use that information to determine whether any given passenger should be flagged as suspicious.

So what are these behaviors? How many are there? How many points are associated with each? We don't know. That information is classified as "sensitive security information." That's one reason it is hard to evaluate the SPOT program.

There are a few hints about the behaviors in the 2010 report. The cues are ones believed to be indicative of stress, fear, or deception. Officers, we are told, are trained to look for and recognize "facial expressions, body language, and appearance that indicate the possibility that an individual is engaged in deception and fears discovery." The checklist does not include indicators that might suggest profiling, such as race, ethnicity, or religion.

If you do get flagged as suspicious, the first thing that will happen is that one of the officers will initiate an informal conversation with you. The officer might make some small talk, ask where you are headed, and so forth. The purpose is to see if there is some obvious reason why you may be behaving suspiciously that does not pose any threat to anyone else (for example, you are headed out of town to have an affair). If the officer is satisfied with your answers, nothing else happens - you are good to go. If you had not read this blog post or the government report, you might not even realize that the conversation was anything but casual.

If the officer is not satisfied with your answers, then you are referred for further screening to another Behavioral Detection Officer and a Transportation Security Officer. If your behavior exceeds some threshold, then you will be referred to a Law Enforcement Officer, who can tap into various data systems, do background checks, and decide whether to make an arrest or clear you for boarding. If you are cleared by that officer, the Transportation Security Officer can still decide that the threat is too great to allow you to board.

So does SPOT work? On April 6, 2011, a Congressional subcommittee held a hearing on that question. It was broadcast on C-SPAN and can be viewed here. According to the proceedings and the written statements submitted by the witnesses, a high-quality study has been conducted and described in a report, but that report has not yet been made publicly available. The yet-to-be-released results are from a base rate study, in which the number of people detained by the SPOT program (and the reasons for which they were detained) was compared to the results of choosing people for screening at random.

The results that were reported in the 2010 report were based on passenger boardings at SPOT airports between 2004 and 2008. The relevant passengers numbered about 2 billion. Of those, about 152,000 were referred for secondary screening. Of those 152,000, about 14,000 were referred to law enforcement officers, and then about 1,100 were arrested. We don't know how many should have been arrested but were missed.

What were the arrests for? The greatest number, 39%, were arrests of people who were undocumented. Next were those with outstanding warrants, 19%, then those who had fraudulent documents, 15%. Another 12% were arrested for a miscellaneous category of reasons that included intoxication and unruly behavior, and an additional 12% were arrested for drug possession. Two other categories each comprised, at most, 1% of the arrests: undeclared currency and documents that were suspect. For a final 1% of the arrests, no reason was recorded.

So where were the arrests of terrorists? There may not have been any. The report estimates that suspected terrorists account for 1 in every 173 million passengers. During the time of the 2004-2008 study, 23 suspected terrorists passed through SPOT airports. However, even in airports that are participating in the SPOT program, behavior detection officers are not stationed at every check-point. The report notes that there was no way of knowing whether the 23 suspected terrorists passed through checkpoints monitored by SPOT-trained officers.

If you want to listen to the subcommittee testimonies or read the written reports submitted by the witnesses, you may want to pay special attention to Professors Maria Hartwig and Paul Ekman, who provide starkly contrasting assessments of the performance and promise of SPOT. It will be interesting to see what we learn from the results of the newer base-rate study.

28.

Can a Computer Tell When You Are Lying?

Machines have detected 5 key cues to spotting liars. But is that good enough?

In my research on the psychology of lying, I have been most interested in the kinds of lying and lie-detection that happened in ordinary life, by people who had no access to any special equipment or expertise. When I ask the question, "Can you tell when someone is lying?" I like to answer it by letting people watch other people (whom I knew to be lying or telling the truth) and tell me their guesses as to those people's truthfulness. I learned that on average, <u>people aren't very good</u> at knowing when other people are lying.

But could a computer do better?

Sure, they don't have the intuition that humans do, but they are also not at risk of the kinds of <u>mistakes</u> that are specific to humans, such as emotional investment in *wanting* to think that a certain person is lying, or that another sort of person <u>would *never* lie to them</u>.

Suppose you could give computers a transcript of the lies and truths that you said, wrote, or typed, and then programmed the machines to look for particular kinds of cues. How would the computers do? Of course, in this sort of approach to lie-detection, computers don't get to make judgments based on your lying eyes (or any other parts of you)—they just have to go by your *words*. Contrary to the conventional wisdom, though, <u>language cues</u> (what we say) offer even more promising clues about deception than do visual nonverbal cues (how we look).

121

The promise of finding accurate computer-based lie-detection has gripped researchers, and dozens have gone on a quest to see if it works. There are computer programs written to find and count relevant linguistic cues in transcripts, and social scientists have used them to see if computers can find any reliable differences in the transcripts of communications *known* to be lies compared to the transcripts *known* to be truths.

The question addressed in these studies is, "Do certain kinds of linguistic cues show up more (or less) frequently when people are known to be lying, compared to when they are known to be telling the truth?"

For a new review article, the authors rounded up <u>44 relevant studies</u>. There were 38 different cues measured in enough of the studies that they could combine all the results and see which cues emerged as reliable and telling clues to deception.

First, I'll give you the best case for the success of the computers. Then I'll tell you why the computers were actually pretty *unimpressive*, much like humans are.

The Best Case for Computers: The Cues to Deception that They Found

Some cues separated the truths from the lies better than others did. In order of the strength of the cues (or magnitude of the effect sizes, for those who prefer the statistical jargon), here are the computer-identified cues to deception:

1. *Liars do not use as many different words as truth-tellers do.* This is called "content word diversity." The results seem to suggest that liars don't access the same range of vocabulary that truth-tellers do. They fall back on the same words rather than using a variety of words.

122

2. *Liars' answers have fewer sentences and fewer words.* Liars just don't seem to have as much to say as truth-tellers do. It is as if they are holding back, or maybe they are so busy trying to remember what to say or what not to say that they end up not saying much at all.

3. *Liars express anger more than truth-tellers do.*

4. *Liars seem to make fewer exceptions than truth-tellers do.* The computers figured this out by counting words such as *except, but,* and *without.* People who are telling the truth make more of these kinds of distinctions than liars do.

5. *Liars distance themselves from what they are saying.* Specifically, compared to truth-tellers, they are less likely to use the first person ("I") and more likely to use the second person ("you") or the third person ("he" or "she" or "they").

The Unenthusiastic Case for Computers as Lie Detectors

Okay, so computers can separate liars from truth-tellers in the five ways I just described. But the authors looked at computers' use of 38 different linguistic cues, and only for *half* of them did the computers find *any* differences that were statistically significant—and some of those differences between lies and truths were very small.

Also, those conclusions I just offered above are based on averages across all of the 44 studies that included those cues. But the 44 studies varied in lots of different ways. For example, in some, the liars and truth-tellers were talking about their own personal experiences—often, emotional ones. In others, they were describing people they liked or disliked. In studies in which people described their own experiences, sometimes they described neutral experiences and other times, they were describing very negative experiences. In some studies, the liars and truth-tellers were typing (as in e-mail communications); other times, they were talking, and still other times they were writing by hand. Sometimes, the liars were highly motivated to get away with their lies, and the truth-tellers really cared about not getting mistaken as liars; other times, it just didn't matter much.

In all, the authors showed results for 15 different variations. You can think of them as different contexts for lying, or different kinds of lies, or different ways of lying, or different feelings about lying—what's important is that these variations matter. Liars lie in different ways in different contexts. For example, liars express more negative emotions (they use more words indicative of anger) than truth-tellers do when they are describing their own personal experiences; but when they are just talking about who they like and dislike, then liars and truth-tellers do not differ in their expression of negative emotions.

Here's something really striking: *There was no one cue to deception that statistically separated the liars from the truth-tellers across all 15 different contexts and types of lies.* The one that came closest was the number of words. For most of the different contexts and types of lies and feelings about lies, the liars had less to say (they said fewer words) than the truth-tellers. Again, though, the results were true for most contexts, but not all.

A perfect cue to deception would be one that occurs *every time* a person is lying, and *never* occurs when someone is telling the truth. The classic example is Pinocchio's nose. But the truth is, there is no Pinocchio's nose. It doesn't matter whether humans are looking for the cues or computers are: They just aren't there.

Reference:

Hauch, V., Blandon-Gitlin, I., Masip, J., & Sporer, S. L. (2015). Are computers effective lie-detectors? A meta-analysis of linguistic cues to deception. *Personality and Social Psychology Review, 19,* 307-342.

29.

Accused of Doing Something Awful? Here's How to Convince Others of Your Innocence

Don't pretend you're perfect – that's not credible.

Amanda Knox is on trial for murder. She insists on her innocence. What could she possibly to do to convince people to believe her?

Back when my primary area of interest was the psychology of deception, I had a terrific graduate student (now a professor) who wanted to answer the question of how people who are accused of a serious offence can establish their innocence. Weylin Sternglanz conducted a series of studies on that question for his dissertation. He never studied people who were accused of murder, so we can't know for sure if his results would generalize to bad behaviors of that magnitude, but his findings are suggestive.

Sternglanz believed that people who completely deny an accusation of serious wrongdoing are not as likely to be believed as those who admit to a lesser offense. Take, for example, the case of academic cheating, as when a student is accused of copying a fellow student's answers on a test. Students who simply deny the accusation are less likely to be seen as innocent than those who say they did not personally engage in cheating but they did see someone else cheat and did not report it.

The cheating example was the basis for one of Sternglanz's studies. In another study, people described times they really were accused of serious transgressions (such as drunk driving, infidelities, plagiarizing, and engaging in nonlethal violence). In that study and one other, people adopted different strategies in their attempts to convince others (all of whom were strangers) of their innocence. The two key strategies were simply denying the accusation and admitting to a lesser offence. Others included for comparison included making a counter-accusation, offering an explanation for the accuser's suspicions, admitting to a lesser offence that had nothing to do with the accusation in question, and not responding to the accusation at all.

Across the three studies, Sternglanz found that people who admitted to a lesser offense were less likely to be judged as guilty than were those who outright denied the accusation. Other strategies varied in their effectiveness, but no strategy was significantly more effective than admitting to a lesser offense.

Sternglanz believes that what is most important is to come across as someone who is basically an honest person. People who admit to small failings are more likely to seem honest than those insist that they did nothing at all wrong.

Reference:

Sternglanz, R. W. (2009). Exoneration of serious wrongdoing via confession to a lesser offence. In M. S. McGlone & M. L. Knapp (Eds.), *The interplay of truth and deception* (pp. 165-192). New York: Routledge.

About the Author

Bella DePaulo (Ph.D., Harvard University) is one of the world's foremost experts on the psychology of lying and detecting lies. Her published work includes some of the most influential and widely-cited articles in the field.

Dr. DePaulo has lectured nationally and internationallyin countries such as Italy, Sweden, Finland, Poland, Wales, the Netherlands, and Canada, as well as the United States. She has given workshops and has addressed criminal attorneys, judges, polygraphers, members of the national intelligence community (such as the CIA and the FBI), physicists, marketing professionals, high school teachers, and medical and mental health practitioners.

Bella DePaulo also writes myth-busting, consciousness-raising, totally unapologetic books on single life. The *Atlantic* magazine has described her as "America's foremost thinker and writer on the single experience." She is the award-winning author of *Singled Out: How Singles Are Stereotyped, Stigmatized, and Ignored, and Still Live Happily Ever After*, and has been writing the "Living Single" blog for *Psychology Today* since 2008. Dr. DePaulo's writings have been published in the *New York Times*, the *Washington Post*, *Time* magazine, and many other places. Her TEDx talk, "What no one ever told you about people who are single," was an instant hit.

After two decades as a Professor of Psychology at the University of Virginia, Dr. DePaulo moved to the west coast in the year 2000 for what was supposed to be a 1-year sabbatical at the University of California at Santa Barbara. She never returned. She is currently an Academic Affiliate in Psychological and Brain Sciences at UCSB. Visit Bella DePaulo's website at BellaDePaulo.com.